SURVIVAL GEAR

Rita Moir

POLESTAR
BOOK PUBLISHERS

Survival Gear
Copyright © 1994 by Rita Moir

Published by:
Polestar Press Ltd.
1011 Commercial Drive, Second Floor
Vancouver, BC
Canada   V5L 3X1

The Publisher would like to acknowledge the
financial assistance of The Canada Council,
British Columbia Cultural Services Branch,
and the Department of Canadian Heritage.

Editing by Julian Ross and Bonnie Evans.
Cover design and illustration by Jim Brennan.
Production by Michelle Benjamin and Julian Ross.
Printed in Canada by Best-Gagne.

Canadian Cataloguing in Publication Data

Moir, Rita
     Survival gear
ISBN 0-919591-81-7
 1. Nova Scotia—Description and travel. 2.
Canada—Description and travel. I. Title.
FC2317.5M64 1994   917.1604'4
C94-910489-2   F1037.M64 1994

To Edwina Crocker and Caroline Woodward

Georgie and Edwina and Parker taught me a phrase I hadn't heard before.

My kids used me good, Georgie said one day down at the Legion with an air of satisfaction. Used him good? I wondered why he was smiling when someone used him.

I didn't understand then the honesty of the transaction. Your kids will use you, as you will use your friends, and they you. You will expect and return favours. There will often be use of a person or a situation, but the use will be good or bad.

He used me bad, I have heard said. Or she used me good.

A person in the village would say to me — come to the funeral, maybe you'll get some material you can use for your stories. Come out on the boat, maybe you can use something.

To the people who have helped me in Freeport, I hope I have used you good.

Thank yous:

In Nova Scotia: Andy Moir, Chris Callaghan, Lloyd, Krystal and Kevin Crocker, Edwina, Cecil and Daniel Crocker, Parker Thurber, Carol Welch, Alain Meuse, Paula Danckert, and the people of Freeport who allowed me their stories.

Across the map: Erin, Ross, Judy, Brian and Donna Moir, the Hallatt family, Heather Brown, Alison Gordon, Errol Bredon, Paul and Margaret Lewis, Ruth Rejno and Mick Lowe.

In British Columbia: Editors Julian Ross, Michelle Benjamin and Bonnie Evans; John Juliani, Jim Sinclair, Ann MacMillan, the teachers and supporters of the Kootenay School of Writing in Nelson who helped me to believe that writing is an honourable job, and to my friends in the Kootenays who keep on keeping on — Corky Evans, T.C. Carpendale, Moe Lyons, Sandy Korman, Sally Mackenzie, Jeff George and Seamus, Marcia Braundy, Sam Simpson, Philip Pedini, Sabbian and Bernie Clover and family, and all the members of the IMAGES Ad Hoc Singers, past and present. Thanks to Joanne Ellis and Margaret Darling for the phrase, Bent pins and broken needles. "Crowing Away the Dark" is the name of a woodcut print by Nancy Pridham of Creston, B.C.

Everywhere, always: Connor, who has been with me every inch of the way, and CBC Radio, for the same.

Survival Gear

My home is in British Columbia

MY HOME IS IN BRITISH COLUMBIA, deep in the Interior forest and mountains, where I cannot see the sky, feel the wind, watch the sun rise and set. At least, that is how it seems sometimes.

My home is in British Columbia, I think. But here by the Bay of Fundy, 3,000 miles from home, it will take months to leave home. Dreams are slow to subside.

Sometimes running means survival.

At home, the grouse pound their wings in the bush behind my house, *whup whup whup whup.* The coyote stands in the dawn light that filters through the lacy green of the larch.

Down the road, there was an Indian blockade. First there weren't any Indians, and then there were, a band once officially deemed extinct returned to prove they weren't, and the neighbourhood blew up. In my home in B.C., everyone takes sides, immediately.

Down the dirt road, in the community hall we have been building for twenty years, there have been too many benefits and work crews and dances in the dark and where are the RCMP when we need them.

Down the long dirt road, a dispute with a neighbour has turned to bile, too many boundaries crossed.

My world has closed in — too many elections in too few years, too many meetings, press releases, disputes.

Finally, an election is won, a relationship ended.

Sometimes flight is survival.

Sometimes survival means ridding yourself of hate.

A friend offers me a free ticket. But I tell her it is the journey I want, not the trip.

✦

I am determined not to save potato water

IT IS HARD TO TRAVEL or have an adventure when you are worrying about potato water. Caring for potato water or the home-butchered chicken, good enough for company back in 1983, is worse than owning a cow. It demands your presence, preparation and plastic containers. Throw it out. It is only fear of the adventure that stops you. If someone tries to prevent you from buying kiwi, give them all your potato water. And a cabbage. And a turnip.

✦

R I T A   M O I R

Tips to travellers crossing Canada
by car in winter

GO AHEAD.

Take an exit.

An entrance.

If you're wrong, you can usually turn back.

Be bold. Give yourself permission to become an authorized vehicle and cross the median.

Use studded radials if you can get away with it.

Carry a shovel, buy heavy jumper cables at Canadian Tire, fill the thermos, bring a water bucket for the dog, and the dog to protect you and be all that's familiar.

In hotel rooms, watch the weather channel. In Winnipeg, my brother Brian is freezing. In Freeport, my brother Andy is freezing. Back home in B.C., my friends are freezing. Our country is unified by cold.

If you have to cry awhile, it's okay. If you have to puke, stop the car if it's safe, and if it isn't, open the window and blast yourself with cold air and snow.

Take pictures of the snow — in the Kootenays, in the coulees of Alberta, on the elevators at Purple Springs, in Kildonen Park where Gramp proposed to Nana by the frozen Red River, in Blind River — then kiss the grass still green in Quebec.

Try ordering your sausages in French. *Les Saucisses*.

Talk to truck drivers. They'll wave to you back on the road after breakfast where you've ordered your sausages in French. Tell people if you're tired or lost. They'll be your guardian angel on the road when your headlight's broken, and through the dark night of New Brunswick they will lead you through the twists and turns of highway they know like you know your own back road back home.

Into Nova Scotia, down the Digby neck, the car drives like it is home.

Remember what it's like to squint in the horizon, hand moving by itself into a salute to the sun?

✦

God damn you Connie Kaldor, Garnet Rogers you make me cry

THE MOUNTAINS ARE FILLING WITH SNOW again. It does not matter if it is winter or spring — this country is impassable. The avalanches make me go the long way, and Garnet Rogers sings *farewell you northern hills, you mountains all goodbye.*

The Crowsnest is snowed in, the highways a mess freezing into transport ruts that will throw you, and the truckers say don't try it, stay in Fernie, the depressed mining town — one day perhaps it will look like Natal and Michel, rebuilt and corporate, where once sooty laundry flapped in the mountains amidst the coal-covered shacks.

Then it's damn you Connie Kaldor in the morning's sun, with the pulse of your outlaw song, packhorse car picking its way through the stony creekbed roads of B.C., sun dogs guiding me, racing through blue sky and gold wheat rolls, thumping and hollering all the way into Alberta and another blizzard that strands me, the snow so thick that I cannot pick my way through the town where I used to live.

✦

Grazyna's pickles

LETHBRIDGE. HERITAGE DRIVE, the new section of town.

It is October 27th, two days away from home and ten days since the election in B.C. Today is the Polish election. I don't know anyone at this table of Polish people except for the old friends who saved me from the storm and brought me here on this cold night.

Outside it is -26.4°C, breaking the record cold of -18°C, set in 1949. The car is parked in deep snow and vicious wind out here near Heritage Drive, in a row of new houses where we once slithered down the coulees, exploring for trilobite and cow bones.

Our hostess is Grazyna. A Polish man kisses me at Grazyna's table. He and the Polish expatriates make jokes. A sort of Polish light bulb joke, you might say. How many Poles, they ask, does it take to make three political parties? Answer: two. Because we have so many factions, you see? Two people, three parties! Even we have a party called Friends of Beer, which we will toast. 150 parties we have in Poland today on election day.

I like the joke. It makes the factions back home in B.C. appear modest. And besides, it is a good joke in the midst of a blizzard. There is candlelight, a fireplace, accents and wine. I have crossed several borders from home, just one province behind me. Polish voices envelop me, take me over like the snow.

We are sitting at Grazyna's table. You arrive at five p.m. You sit. Five is when the food is served. We are eating and drinking, much wine and vignac. We are eating from cream-coloured plates with scalloped edges and roses twining through them. Pork, breaded and fried; cabbage, boiled with salt and pepper and bay leaves, stirred with crisp bacon and the taste of vinegar. We are eating beets, pickled and mashed, and Grazyna's dills. We are eating cucumber, carrot and potato soup, boiled potatoes, pears, celery and carrot salad, fruit salad with kiwi, chocolate cake and more pickles. Grazyna's pickles. She gave me the recipe if you want it.

Some people here at Grazyna's table do not speak English. Some do not speak Polish.

The Polish man and woman brought the vignac from Poland. They are visitors. She is a famous biologist who, with my old friend, Paul, spends her Sunday afternoons in the biology lab in the stressed concrete university killing baby chicks they have infected with leucochloridium parasites. It is a rarefied and rare experiment. The chicks are killed humanely, with gas. Stressed concrete I find depressing on a Sunday afternoon. Snow drifts in hard eddies against the metal grey wolves outside the glass, in that long corridor in the coulees, with the wind soughing along the carpets the colour of ripe and drying grasses.

Out there it is cold, but in here, at Grazyna's table, we are steadied by the fire, the firelight on wine glasses, and huddle closer as we're buffeted by stories from foreign lands.

The Polish man, through the vignac, say it, *vignac*, like cognac, but it is vignac, tells me tales stranger and stranger, through the deep amber liqueur and the Polish voices and the brush of the thigh he tells me he was Polish attaché on an international commission. He is worldly, with grey at the temples, and speaks many languages. He talks about Vietnam and exotic foods.

I squint at him through my glass of vignac, as Grazyna writes out her recipe for pickles. It is not like recipes I have known. Grazyna's dills, like the stories, come from another place. They include the root of horseradish, and the seeds of green peppercorns.

Snow and wind scream in the night. I am uncertain of the road tomorrow. I may never taste vignac again. Or these pickles. Or these stories. I accept each offer of more.

The shape-shifting has begun.

✦

Pink and prairie morning

UP AT 6:15, A PERFECT COLD PINK and prairie morning. The Weather Network, Channel 30, sounds the all clear from Lethbridge, roads so cold and clean you can drive 120 on the melted straights, fields of gold stubble poke up through the white dusting, drivers smiling, released from the storm. The shape-shifting is over. The vertical and horizontal lines of the prairies are reliable again. The grey-blue elevators at Purple Springs reassure me by saying Purple Springs right on them in large letters. I stop to take a picture, can see for miles in the bright prairie sun on new snow.

I find a postcard that quotes the French architect Le Corbusier, who described grain elevators as the "Cathedrals of the Canadian Prairies." I buy the small Saskatchewan newspapers and read about the election. My party has won here, too.

Today could be a thousand miles. Maybe even Winnipeg.

By 4:00 in the afternoon I have passed Regina. Winnipeg is only another 556 kilometres, and the road is clean and fast.

My dog, Connor, is in the back, relaxed on the long strip of foam rubber with the sleeping bag open for him.

He naps during the long rolling parts, sits up when the gears shift, or when I roll down the window for a blast of cold air and the smell of snow. We've made a pact on this trip. We can only do this if he generally pays attention, and if I generally trust him. The dog will not take a shit on a leash — he is too discreet. He needs some privacy. And there are too many days of this country to cross without letting him run. He will understand the tone of my voice when I am not joking, when there is no leeway any more, and I will understand that he can sense danger, for himself and for me. We will rely on each other for protection and friendship. And for romps in the snowy parks together along the way.

Skirling snow on the dark prairie road begins to mock us, like a Calvinist preacher, as if we have been taking life too easy. I turn down the radio. Sit up straight. Concentrate. Alert extra ancient senses to the shrieking of the wind. Get out of here, it says, you're off limits. Out of bounds. Pushed — knocked broadside, studs grab the road again. Push, watch it. You're outside your jurisdiction, it says. You've forgotten the wind. There will be no Winnipeg tonight. The dog tenses, looming in the back, blocking my rear view. Lie down, I scream at him. He understands. Lies down.

White hoods us, blocks even the tail lights of semi trailers, the lighthouses of the prairies. The road narrows to a path. Moosomin 11 kilometres. Either creep to the side and end up on the news, or hold course, radio off, heater down, all noise minimized but the wind. Listen and drive. At the first lights of Moosomin, snow stripping and whipping up to the streetlights, I veer into the motel parking lot and drive straight for the office. Two stunned faces peer out the round spot they have scrubbed in the frosted window. The man steps outside. I have missed their entrance by 50 metres, tanked over the snowed-in curb and into their fence of sawed-off railway ties planted vertically in the horizontal earth. Couldn't see it. All reliable lines are hidden again.

✦

Brenda

SHE GIVES ME A PROFILE over a glass of white wine, as she shrugs off her coat and twists to arrange it behind her at The Classic, the restaurant across from the Moosomin Motel. Her nails are long and painted, too long for waitressing or gardening, typing or factory work. She wears four rings. Her hair is long, too, with glints of red. She's from Calgary and talks about real estate. She's 29 to my 39. She arrived five minutes after me, booked room 132 next to mine. She's travelling alone, the same route as me, with her dog and her cat, in her four-wheel drive. Has to be in the Sault by tomorrow, then back to Calgary to have her nose re-broken.

I broke my nose in softball ten years ago, eh? she says over her shrimp salad.

I played softball once too, at an NDP fundraiser. Scraped my hands and knees when I tripped on my way to first.

Her four-wheel drive is a big Bronco with a bright pink racing stripe. Mine is an old Toyota with a black stripe. Her dog is a Pekinese. Mine is big and black. Her cat, slender and tawny, crawls forward across the seats. Brenda's coat is fox fur. Mine is black cotton, like an old Russian greatcoat. I feel my Prairie sullenness move in, stocky, cranky, shove my hands into my pockets, glower and cross the street when the light turns green, always carry a shovel in the car, wear plain clean cotton underwear.

She picks at her shrimp while I plough into the chips and gravy.

Imagine, getting your nose broke in softball.

In my motel room, next to hers, I pick up *Safe at Home*, a baseball mystery by Alison Gordon. The wind screams and pounds against the aluminum frame windows. At night I dream of a man I knew. You're getting married, right? I say to him in the dream, at the coffee shop. Yes, and you wouldn't believe, he says sheepishly, how traditional our rings are. He puts his hand on my back. I remove it.

And then in the morning, when Brenda and I are both huffing and snorting in the cold, shovelling our 4x4s out of the drifts, and I've let my dog off his leash, she keeps saying where's your dog, where's your dog, he's going to get run over, where is he I can hear him jingling. I say, mind your own damn dog, try to act like I'm not worried, give Connor a whistle and miraculously he returns and in a regal exit we sweep out into another prairie storm 20 kilometres down the road toward Brandon.

I'm back on my old familiar highway that I must navigate by orange markers placed along the ditch, like buoys on my way to the ocean.

✦

Cross the median

I LEARN THAT I DO NOT KNOW how to make an entry into a city. I remain on the fringe of Montreal, huddled where I will not get lost again, not because of the French, but because the traffic is heavy in the Friday night dark and the dog head loomed in the mirror, and I went in circles and circles until I arrived here at this motel beneath the Champlain Bridge. I do not have alcohol as an entry into the night of the city. Instead, I watch the weather network, get up to another pink dawn to drive in one day to the ferry at Saint John. I comprehend that what I do is keep going. I castigate myself for not seeking adventure, but think perhaps later that the journey is what I will understand. Again I get turned in the wrong direction. I curse viciously, bear down and swing the car across the median, and squeal into the correct lane.

✦

Arrival

IN MY HOME OF BRITISH COLUMBIA, the trees hide
the view sometimes. I have no generations of aunts and
grandmothers and uncles and fathers and mothers to
help my vision. There is nothing to fall back on. There
is no set way of doing things. There is a drain on the
store of wisdom and a stuttering rhythm to the endur-
ance we must find in a crisis.

I have never been to Nova Scotia before. But my
brother Andy and his partner Chris Callaghan are here
on this island in this village called Freeport. There are
traditions and family here and I need that right now.

It is the weekend. Andy and Chris are here from
their working life in Halifax. They know when to watch
for me from the veranda because the ferry traffic comes
down Long Island at the same time every hour. As I
drive down the island, 14 kilometres from the top to the
bottom, I see forests of small tough spruce, houses
strung along the road, and sometimes catch a glimpse
of the ocean. As I drive over the last rise, Crocker's Hill,
I see the Bay of Fundy, the village, the white spire of the
church, and large expanses of grass like a prairie. I see
sky forever. I can feel my lungs opening, like a bellows
that has been closed too long.

I have come here for two weeks, but stay for ten months, alone during the week while Andy and Chris are across the province at work.

I learn that for some young people, the tradition here scratches their skin. They want the smell of fish out of their clothes. But this tradition allows me to be still, to listen and learn from people whose families have been here hundreds of years.

In this spot in Nova Scotia, they still dig the graves by hand, as we have learned to do back home, but here they have always done it that way. Large families run back centuries. They don't have to make up all the songs, the harmonies. Stories are known and repeated.

✦

The rat and chickens story

GEORGIE CROCKER'S AT THE Freeport Legion. His Dad Harry got buried today up on the hilltop next to all the other Crockers. Georgie hadn't seen his Dad for seven years. Not since the accident. Not the one where his Dad was hunting and shot off part of his forehead and had to crawl out of the woods alone. No, the other accident, later, where he got knocked off his scooter into the ditch by a car, and no one ever knew who did it. After that Harry didn't want Georgie to see him any more, wanted his son to remember him the way he was before. Some kind of pact Harry asked for long ago.

It looks like Harry from here, from this angle, says a family member in the white Baptist church where Harry lies for viewing. She shifts me closer to Harry's face, where the old gunshot scar has been filled in above the left temple.

There's some real flowers in the church, but mostly they're plastic and cloth, propped on tripods, they're the ones that last up in the wind off the Atlantic in March on the hilltop. The flowers get sent down in the hearse from Digby.

I remember that time we had all those chickens, 300 of them, and jeez, I still like chicken, Georgie says later, down at the Legion, pulling at the label of his beer. Three hundred of them we had, and every night they all goes into the pen there, the chicken coop. But when they comes out in the morning, Dad sees some's just walking around on their stubs, and Georgie curls all his fingers, the ones that aren't permanently bent under from the time his arm got crushed between the boat and the wharf, and stumps his knuckles to the centre of the table, just like this, the chickens are on their stubs, he says, just like this. Just stubs. And Dad says, by the sweet Jesus, what's happening with these chickens, they got no toes. No toes, he says.

So Dad, he's gonna find out just what's going on, can't have no 300 chickens walking around on their stumps, where're those toes getting to? So he gets his gun and he goes out to the henpen that night. And he sets. And he sets. And nothing happens. So he sets some more. Sets there with the chickens. Waiting. And it's getting about dawn and he's setting there, right sleepy, when he sees it. A nose. A nose sticking up through the floorboards, a nose. It's a rat, and Georgie thrusts his nose up in the air and sniffs, just a poking his nose up at all those hens' toes. That rat's looking at some nice dinner, how many toes is that, 300 hens? Quite a few toes. So Dad he takes his rifle and he shoots that rat right in the nose. There, he says, and Georgie laughs and walks his knuckles across the table again. Jeez, that was some good dinner that rat was getting for a while there, and he curls his hands onto his belly and laughs, swiping back the locks of his new haircut he got for the funeral.

✦

If I could save time in a bottle

MORE USE IS MADE OF THE Westport library than any other library in Nova Scotia. That's what a study about Brier Island says. Brier Island is the next island over.

The librarian teaches children age four how to glue and tape coloured paper in links for the Christmas tree. A crew of seven on a government work project repairs the front steps. Daniel Crocker, Edwina and Cecil Crocker's son, finishes gluing his paper chain and reaches for the wooden model of *Spray,* the Grand Passage ferry we've just crossed on from his home of Freeport.

Daniel is related to nearly everyone in Freeport, and many here in Westport. If he's not related to everyone in his village of 472 people, everyone knows him anyway and watches out for him. Cars and trucks slow down to see who's walking with Daniel. If you want to meet people you've never met, go for a walk with him.

Daniel will be a fisherman, just like his Dad Cecil and his uncles Lloyd and Earl and their cousin Georgie are fishermen. He points to the painted markers on the water, they are "booeys" not "boys". He says "boat" and it sounds like "bout".

31

Daniel likes books on boats, books about lobstering, and the librarian finds them. She knows Daniel and knows that two years ago his brother Isaac died when Daniel was a baby. Her own son died in Daniel's uncle Earl's arms, a hunting fatality. She is teaching the kids how to make links for the Christmas tree.

Daniel's brother Isaac died when he was two years old. He crawled up on the table and drank from a bottle of oil of wintergreen, the liniment all fishing families once kept in store for taking the cold out of sea-bitten hands. Isaac is buried in the cemetery above the bay, behind his family's home, up with the gulls, over the water where his father and uncles go lobstering, in the graveyard where his mother Edwina spent a summer forcing back the alder while Daniel, his red hair damp and curly, just like his father's, slept in the car or played by the stone for his brother Isaac, the stone that says, If I could save time in a bottle.

That January Edwina conceived a new child, but it was just a trick her body played on her because she wanted so much to create life again; in the hospital ten weeks after conception, the nurse showed her the piece of tissue like a deformed cauliflower that they'd removed from her and placed in a bottle, and Edwina said it didn't fizz her any and she started again, and Amos was born at the end of the next cold February.

Daniel is out in the driveway, wrestling with the dog over bait bags amidst the lobster traps. Edwina fills the bait bags from vats of salted herring in the new shed they built. No, it doesn't smell, no matter what the one neighbour says. Everyone else says it's fine. Ten cents a bag, she'll fill a thousand for the first day of lobster, November 25, the slimy decomposing fish that don't smell so bad if the door's open and there's a good breeze. The smell of money, they say down at the Scotiabank, and the post office, especially on Wednesday, pay day at D.B. Kenney's fish plant.

The fishermen impale the bags on the spike in the lobster trap. Daniel's father Cecil and his uncle Lloyd are down at the boat, preparing for the 7 a.m. opening, the dark and cold of night in Atlantic November. The traps are rarely wood anymore, they're metal, green, and don't smash up or rot. Each boat uses a different coloured buoy, bright pink, oranges, blue. No getting beered up now. Fishing starts. Early to bed. No one knows the price. They never know until a week into lobster. The talk has it up to $4 a pound. Within the week, Daniel's parents know it's only $2.50 a pound, not $4, and Christmas is coming. In Halifax, a lobster dinner, a one-pound lobster, with potato salad, sells for $21.95.

All these families, all Daniel's uncles and cousins, all the fishing families of southwest Nova Scotia, tie up their boats. They've talked in meetings, on the wharf, at the Legion, on the VHF, on the phone and ferries. It's their first strike, and without a union.

And Daniel will be a fisherman. He finishes gluing his paper chain and opens the books on boats.

✦

Grass fires

DID YOU SEE THE GRASS FIRE down at the swamp last night?

Yes, Edwina says as she shifts Amos on her hip and slips her CBC Halifax coffee cup into the microwave.

It reminds me of home in the Kootenays, I say. Every spring the old people love to burn. Makes me homesick.

We had grass fires in the spring too, Edwina says. Even us little kids got to help. Everyone stood in a circle, and all you could see is the fire — the whole swamp on fire — silhouettes, people standing there together, leaning on their pitchforks, and the smoke and sparks and the stars.

I'd feel that heavy waterpack on my back and then go squirt at the edges of the fire and the pack would get lighter and lighter, she says, and I wondered if I wanted to go back for more. One spring mum lit the field on fire and it headed for the spruce trees uphill and she yells at me, go fill the waterpacks Edwina! and I was refilling them in the middle of the living room, water on the floorboards, while I'm phoning all the families I can think of for help, and my mum says, why're you on the phone.

People will come to a grass fire to help, Edwina says, giving Amos his bottle. It's like anything, they've got to see something happening. It's got to be visual.

And she said, it used to be the people in this village who are old now took care of everything, started all the new things around here when they were young. All the stuff for the community. It was the Rebekkahs and the Oddfellows and the Masons then. They organized the fires and they started the choirs, and they brought in wood for widows and they built the community hall. They sat with the sick and grieving, and they dug the graves. Sort of like you're trying to do back at your home in B.C. They did it all for years, and they got tired.

Then it kind of skipped a generation. It was stagnant, the old way or no way, no new ideas came in, and nobody saw anything happening. We lost the doctor, and there was nothing for the kids, and people let things go.

And then Edwina talked about the summer she spent up at the hilltop cemetery, for her own solace, after her little boy Isaac died. She was up there cleaning out the alder and the briar because the graveyard looked like hell and everyone knew it. First, people drove by watching her. She was a curiosity. Then they stopped, and found the graves of their own families, Thurbers and Pynes and Primes, Outhouse and Titus, the stones falling down in the long grass, cracked by the wind or by target practice.

And when she asked for help, they came, like the

neighbour with his bush hog who wouldn't take a cent for the use of his equipment.

It happened again when they wanted to build a village playground. When people saw Edwina and three other pregnant women and 16 kids working on it, even though some people said it would never happen, they did come to help. It was visual.

People get discouraged, she says, but they get kind of pent-up, too. They want things to happen, be part of something.

Like when she chaired her first meeting, with people from all the three villages — trying to work together to bring a doctor back to live here. A lot of people showed up, and some were mad CBC was there, and the resident nurse who was too burned out started yelling at people, and the visiting doctor said how could they expect to attract a physician if they didn't stock fresh lettuce on the island, and some people said he should never have been invited to speak and Edwina said people have got to understand that's the kind of attitude we're dealing with here.

And when it got out of hand, everyone yelling at each other, Edwina stood up there, in front of her community, the people who had come into her home when Isaac died, washed her dishes, made her take a walk by the sea, these people so geared into her feelings, she stood there and said, There's no one here knows better than me the love this community has to give and what it can offer so let's calm down here and figure things out.

And when she and Cecil loaded up the red and white 4x4 Dodge truck with photos and ocean charts and brochures about Freeport, and headed through the storm 200 miles to Halifax to the medical fair, everyone knew about it. They could picture Edwina and Cecil there having a good time in the city, and maybe luring a doctor out to the islands.

Then to cap it off, Andy was going to give them a tour of CBC. But in rush hour traffic they got turned backward in the one-way streets near Citadel Hill, could even see the CBC building in the distance, and then they heard the siren behind them and the cop got out and said, Are you lost? and Cecil with his tattoos and red curls said no, we ain't lost. We can see where we're going just fine, we's just havin' trouble getting there. And Edwina, with her black hair and freckles, smiles at the cop and says, just point us to the ocean and we'll drive down and end it all, and the cop laughed and gave them an escort right through the traffic and everyone down home knew about it before they even left the city. It's the kind of thing everyone could just visualize.

◆

The best people have their fingers cut off

GEORGIE'S SISTER, HEATHER, joins our table at the Legion dance. Tonight's a semi-formal dress code. Heather wears a gown of aqua taffeta and stiff scratchy lace. She's a boisterous blonde who'd look more comfortable in a worn-soft black and green lumberjack shirt. Maybe that's what she was wearing when she cut off her little finger down to the first knuckle. Caught her left hand in the wood splitter. Cut clean. The diamond rings sparkle on the two fingers next to the stump. No trying to hide.

We'd been talking about drug smuggling and that rusty vessel we saw down the French Shore today that looked like an old drug runner, and Cecil's brother, Lloyd, said no one on his dragger better ever use bloody drugs, and no he'd never tried them though he had to admit he got pretty fond of morphine that time he put the axe into his kneecap, and he hauls up his left pantleg there at the table and the night beckons more stories.

Why don't you ever come down home no more, Cecil says, turning to me as my brother Andy starts telling his story to Chris and to Lloyd. What's my brother saying?

Cecil leans over to me, I keep asking Edwina why you don't come down home to visit us more often, he says, we's just watching movies at night. Don't you stay up in that big house alone at night, no reason to be lonely when Andy and Chris is away, you just come on down home.

My brother is talking about the day he cut his finger off.

I asks Edwina, is she mad at us, I says to her a thousand times, why don't she come down home more, and I reassure him no, not ever would I be mad at them and think about the first and only time I heard my brother's story, while Cecil repeats the invitation over and over again, in that Nova Scotia way that means the conversation never stops.

What happened to your hand, I asked just once, 15 years ago in a restaurant in Winnipeg, over a plate of fish and chips.

Didn't you know about that, my brother said, moving his hand out of sight, and leaving no room for questions. It didn't hurt that much, he called the ambulance and went back to the basement workshop to the table saw to look for the piece where the knot of oak exploded in the blade and blew half his left middle finger off, blood on the walls, oak shrapnel ripping into his leather safety apron. Called the ambulance and left a note at home saying where he'd gone. That was about it.

I've hardly seen my brother since then. We used to

play guitar and sing together, but that ended even before the finger. The finger just meant that it wouldn't happen again. Guitars put away. Conversation ended. Full stop. In Manitoba, the less said the better.

Back home in B.C., when Corky cut his finger off, we didn't have an ambulance. Just a bunch of frightened and confused people on the party line, 25 miles from the hospital, all of us with our first aid tickets, even a doctor visiting nearby, and we couldn't get organized. Within minutes everyone was yelling at each other, we got it all wrong, and someone else drove Corky and his finger to the hospital where they stitched it back on, sent him away with a bandage, and left it to rot, and he had to get it cut off anyway. We don't talk about that story a lot yet.

But my brother is telling his story again, the table saw, the note he managed to write, and I can just hear it, softened by kerosene lights and friends and the drone of Cecil's invitation. The story is hardly different from my memory of it. The point is the repetition. The hand in full view.

Edwina says the pain is never gone. It can always be picked open. The loss of a baby, the loss of a finger. It's just that these things were a long time ago, and you don't go down as deep. The wounds are no longer raw. They're not even hidden. They're just there, like the stretch marks telling of a birth.

✦

Bad days, swell days

ON THE BAD DAYS, when the sky comes down to meet the swells, when the wind blows at 60 to 80 kilometres for the eleventh day, and the fishing fleet hasn't been out for as long, and the men lie at home and watch the afternoon movie, and the kids have runny noses, and the women look down at the floor; on those days when the car's gone dead and house locks freeze with salt water, on those days the only amusement — the only thing that makes me smile, is that the wind is so strong the water bobs in the toilet. On those days I draw the curtains at 5:00, push them into the sills to keep out the wind, with its chill of 37 below, and I take out the small TV, its antenna smashing the empty flower vase off the window sill, glass slivering into the sink, the washed dishes, into the hall, and I turn away, turn on *Golden Girls*. This is the dead of winter. The brain dead. The drained dead. Our batteries so low that even a fight is a charge.

✦

Ozone scare

HOW CAN THEY TELL US not to go out in the sun?

My hair itches, there is not one piece of cloth I want to touch my body, I have coughed for weeks, I look in my closet, then in the drawers, then in the closet and again in the drawers, not one thing there can bring me summer, though some days I put on sandals and sailcloth shirt over loose bluejeans, and stay in them until I am driven back to long johns.

How can they tell us to stay inside when the sun finally comes, or to time our moments by an exposure meter. There are only two months when we can lay our bodies on the rocks, be absolutely certain of heat, recharge our bones, stuff the long underwear in the furthest deepest corner, run in and out and in again, no stopping at the door for boots, no listening to the radio for warnings, no tassels caught in zippers, no charred wood singeing the space between the eyes, no fear on the highway, no ache from holding in, conserving, preserving.

Who are they to say we must scrimp now in summer, tighten up, manage. My skin is so confined I want to rip off all layers and go scream naked at the Atlantic, crazy woman, scream my lungs back at it, summer is coming, blow your hardest, these winds will be warm again, and I'll bare my bones to yours, make gentleness for a while, relax the exasperation, the dried-out scratching psoriasis of winter.

How dare they say this, when the doorlatch is frozen and I'm standing outside with pale pink tomatoes freezing in their white plastic container in a white plastic bag in the snowbank and I grab the shovel from the car and whang it against the goddamn latch, drag in another four-foot length of firewood and buck it on the table saw because the chainsaw won't start.

Who are these people who dare to tell me that the sun is not my friend?

◆

Survival gear

LLOYD STRAINS INTO THE YELLOW SLICKER and coveralls, my brother's present to me for my 40th birthday. He tightens the velcro ankle tabs around his slick black pointed go-to-the-party shoes. In a small room away from the party, I help him with the coverall straps.

I'll get Cecil, you watch, he says. I'll tell him it's survival gear.

Lloyd parades before the video camera — it's a joke with him and his brother Cecil, about wearing survival gear on the water. Cecil swears he has survival gear, but mostly it hangs in the hallway of his house, except on cold days he wears it out lobstering. Lloyd says that's no survival gear, he knows because he took the training for it, and how to get it on in 30 seconds or you get kicked into the pool, the cold Atlantic, without it. They're pouring over new charts of the Bay of Fundy, St. Mary's Bay, Georges Bank, that Chris brought from Halifax, and they complain about the change from fathoms to metric, the charts anchored with a plate of chocolate chip cookies and glasses of Scotch my brother Andy keeps filled on the blue-checked tablecloth.

Cecil and Lloyd laugh and bicker, point out where

44

they steamed to on Georges Bank in Lloyd's scallop dragger, *Krystal Anne,* and the fuel pump went on the engine and they had to be rescued in the hurricane, and the tow lines breaking again and again and they thought they'd had it. No survival suits then. Oh well, can't swim anyway. But no, they don't take chances. Don't go out on bad days — they've learned that in southwest Nova Scotia you don't.

In Newfoundland that night, two men in a plane go down en route to Reykjavik. They've carried flares, a raft with a tent, survival suits.

And while these brothers sit at the table, saying survival suits are no good if you can't get them on, and Cecil can't swim anyway, and then about the time Cecil's dragger engine caught on fire down in Beautiful Cove and you never saw a woman move as fast as Edwina down to the shore, I want to kick them, scream at them, I remember Randy Morrison, 17 hours in the Pacific, he lived in his survival suit, no that's not the Atlantic, but he was a fisherman too and we wrote about him in our newspaper and our poetry, and he lived to go home to Prince Rupert. His shipmates, unsuited, didn't.

I want to grab the cookies from your hands, slash through your brotherly charm, call you fucking idiots, but I don't live on the water. My window looks at the sea. I am not of the fishing families whose windows face away — who wants to face the factory after working there all day? It is not beautiful. Instead, go to the Legion, no windows inside, and talk with Georgie. Remember that time we was to Toronto, jeez, that was some time we had. Didn't do nothing bad though, did we? No. We learned to use the buses soon enough, jeez we had some bad time with that taxi. He charges us $50, and my aunt was some mad, she says that's a dollar-fifty bus ride. Yeah, we got done some bad, but live and learn, isn't that right. But jeez, you see what they call fresh fish there? Georgie and me, we's at the market there, you tell it Georgie, you tell'em that time we's at the market there. That woman buying the fish, you tell'em. And Georgie, father of five, he looks up with blue eyes under long bangs and smiles. We's down to the market, just looking at what they sell for fish, and I looks at this pollock, they calls it bluefish down there, and I looks at it and it winks at me, and I says, that's some fresh, yep that's some fresh fish all right, it's winking, then I looks closer and my jeez, it's a maggot, that's a maggot walking in its eye and it looks like it's blinking! By jeez, that's some fresh all right. And this woman's looking to buy it, and I say what're you gonna do with that fish, and she says, I'm gonna cook it and eat it. By jeez, I tells her, I wouldn't feed that to my cat. A maggot! By jeez what them fellers down there call fresh fish.

✦

Cultivator

IN THE PICTURE, Parker is wearing oilskins. Getting oiled up, Georgie calls it.

You can tell from the style of the photo on Parker's end table that it's a long time ago. The colours are more sober than pictures now. The lobster traps are the old wooden kind, the oilskins a duller green.

Parker limps to the kitchen cupboard. One of his ankles is swollen. This has to do with his heart, and the retention of fluids. He opens a glass door, and extracts from the exact spot where he keeps it, the dull green book. It is pocket-size, like a miniature from Alice's Wonderland. It used to fit in his shirt pocket. This is his union membership book from five decades ago, 1945. Canadian Fishermen's Union, East Atlantic Coast, Local 19, initiation fee $5, dues $1. Parker M. Thurber, written back then with black fountain pen, is fading to blue in a book that is older than me.

I turn the small pages with some reverence. I have worked for the United Fishermen and Allied Workers Union on the west coast, and now the fishing fleet here is joining the Maritime Fishermen's Union.

People think this is the first union, this one they're joining now, Parker says. But we had another union 50 years ago. It just didn't last.

The words in Parker's book are not ones I see often now, not anywhere.

... Whatever belongs to one member belongs to all ... to gain fair and just remuneration for his labour, and to gain sufficient leisure for mental cultivation and physical recreation ...

Parker watches me reading the book, and knows where my sympathies lie.

The winter I was 16, he says, it was cold with the wind off the water. We were loading the ice houses for 15 or 20 cents an hour. We walked off the job after a week. This was in the 1930s. Somehow I got elected spokesman and went in and negotiated for 30 cents an hour. That was my first time, and I learned that if you're going for something, go in a decent way first, with your homework done. And then if you don't get it, well, you go harder.

I've represented both sides at the table, union and management, and sometimes it got ugly. Very ugly on both sides. When I got on the school board, we negotiated with the bus drivers. The island here didn't hold with the union. The islanders wanted their kids to go to school. Too many people here never got their school. And then I got a threat put to me on the phone, and let me tell you, there were a lot of people out to meet the bus drivers with baseball bats. I'm telling you, it was ugly all round.

There were times I sided with the student council

against the administration, or I'd stand up there at a school event, and tie into the parents. I'd go down to the school whenever the kids called me. And I'm getting my payback now. Kids I don't recognize — they remember me. I can talk to them, give them advice. Not ugly, just with a smile.

Yes, I've been for the union and sometimes against the union. And I been opening my mouth about things before there ever was a union.

Go ahead, take that book home with you. I'll know where it is when I need it.

✦

RITA MOIR

Christmas in Freeport

WE HAVE A DARK SPRUCE, cut from the hilltop over the bay, but we have no Freeport angel.

We have a painted goose egg and bits of sea shell, Christmas tree lights and gold rivets on string, but our tree needs an angel.

Andy heads for his workshop, Chris for her sewing basket, and I tinker for trinkets.

We meet back at the kitchen table and on the blue-checked tablecloth make our own angel.

The Freeport angel is carved from white styrofoam, the kind discarded in the bay. Her eyes are green glass broken and rolled smooth on the tides below the fish plant, the skin drooping over her wizened right eye, her hair red yarn, shoulder-length, parted strictly down the middle, spraying out over earrings of yellow-breasted toucans perched in tropical leaves. The southern birds gaze along her rouged cheekbones up to her emerald eyes. Her face is flat, her eyebrows pencilled, lips a thin smile that has tasted the oceans from Buenos Aires to the Bay of Fundy, the old sea trading routes, rum and fish and bolts of cloth — her dress a faded patchwork that still lifts some spark from her hair.

The Freeport angel is Pippi Longstocking gone to

sea, her father long dead, she is middle-aged now, her chinline broad and flattened, we can still see her hair in pigtails, Pippi on the beach, Pippi lost, Pippi fighting pirates, Pippi finding home again.

The Freeport angel is not made of straw, she is not angelic, she does not glow or shine through fine-spun angel's hair, she is not pastel. She sits on a bow of dark island spruce, tough as the island wind, she is a lookout on a spar. She is red and green and black, framed by red lights like beacons saying you're almost home.

✦

The day the ceiling fell in

LATE AT NIGHT, I turn on the staircase light again and tiptoe down to the living room. The slabs of broken plaster are gone. Lloyd and Cecil and I shovelled them, soaked and broken, into a wheelbarrow and dumped them out of sight off the front steps. Washed the floor twice even though it was still swollen, get the plaster dust out before it dries into the grain, oak buckled like the swells of the sea. The water pipe soldered, the fire straining to dry the room, the windows steamy, chairs upside down balanced close against the water heaters, the chair Georgie Crocker held court in, its legs and arms propped by tuna fish tins to leave air for draining and drying, the leaves of the Nova Scotia bird books locked together, each bird body ripping if the book is touched. All the first aid is done. Elevate, immobilize, keep warm and dry. Do no more damage.

The floor is drying. Old boat ribs were made from oak, weren't they? Alone in the house, no wind tonight, calm, I kneel at the centre of the floor, where the long strips of yellow oak move in closer to its heart, wood raised from water, I kneel down, smooth it, talking, everything will be okay.

Edwina had moved the organ into the next room,

to dry ground. But it was too late.

The stops of the Berlin organ, white and round, with letters in the old biblical script, *vox angelica, violetta, dolce, diapason,* are stuck, the ivory keys warped, the carved lattice panels a sick grey, staved in from water, the maroon cloth on the foot pumps shredded from age and use, won't give now, no air in these lungs. This is what hurts. The ceiling, the floor, they can be sanded, polished, plastered. But the organ is my brother's voice, the gift of a friend that gave him music in his hands again, where on a late summer night, the hymns, the hymns in this family long-gone from Anglican and Catholic, keep some faith. The music rolls down the hillside through the grasses to the church and the cove, where the minister steps outside to listen.

When my brother finally arrives, to see the old organ, I cannot look at him, I still think it will be better, maybe can be fixed. I've seen it open over the weeks, the doors begin to slide, the keys move, the warping wood gaping, then begin to close. I leave him alone.

Should we build a fire, Andy asks later and we do. And I leave him there.

My brother takes a chair, turns it upright, sits back in the empty room, watches the fire.

Should we put it back as it was, he asks later, and we do, Chris and Andy and I, the rugs and chairs now dry, the morning glories faded and stained, pin the red cloth back on the rocker, roll the organ back into its place against the cracking wall, but at least it is in the room with us now. The cat's basket goes back on the chair. The fire helps. And if you don't look up too high, or down too low, you won't see the disfiguring in the room. Except that after awhile, that's okay too, like the cut-off finger, the real part that tells the story.

By the staircase, two feet from where the pipe burst, an electric piano borrowed from a neighbour remained untouched by water. Chris and Andy plug in the piano, borrow the old organ's swivel seat from its spot in front of the foot pumps, push the piano's program for pipe organ, then rhumba and tango and reggae into the night.

✦

Unfit

FELIX BELZYK HOLDS BACK, too tight, clings to the hill, Kurt Browning, so ready in flaming orange, lurches to the ice. I pull the hot-water bottle and the four-inch screen closer, and Isabelle Brasseur flops on the double axle. Everyone is off stride. Hesitating.

The groaner moans on the ocean. Wind shakes the house, rattles the windows, an irregular screaming scraping my codeined brain, lungs straining too close to pneumonia.

Downstairs, the floor lies warping, furniture shoved aside, a mausoleum.

In the Alice Munro book beside me, the *Progress of Love*, in the story "Fits", the rural woman pushes through the snowdrifts to deliver eggs, to find her neighbour has killed his wife then blown his own head off — a kind of winter fit. In the village, people huddle from the cold, asking why. The man had money worries, some said. Health problems, said others.

In Albertville, Olympian couples, slender and taut, embrace, pair up. Beside me, my dog stinks of grease and marrow from the bone he's been sucking.

When the phone rings, I want to crawl deeper under the covers, unfit for human consumption.

Rappie pie, he says. You want to come down? This man who with his brother removed the caved-in ceiling, brought me bread and scallops, helped haul in the firewood, phoned to check if I was alright, he's asking for my company. Rappie pie, he says. *Paté a la Rapure*, Acadian, soupy, hot, potatoes and turkey, a steaming kitchen. Rappie pie, rapure, rapport.

We're awkward, no ceiling plaster or firewood to fuel the conversation.

There was a man on the island killed himself today, he said. Shot himself. Why, I ask. Some people thought he might have been depressed. Or maybe it was his job.

We're silent awhile and I think about Alice Munro's story, then sit in his kitchen grinning while he flaps the dish towel under the smoke alarm screaming about the burnt spot on the rappie pie, and Krystal bounces in yelling, hey Dad, what's for supper?

◆

Recipe for a winter night

LET GO. If you take a wrong exit you can usually return to your original course.

Let's go to the Legion, shut out winter in the windowless hall down hidden from the wind, where the lights are low and the smoke is thick and we swirl in the Paul Jones; men and women in opposite circles all holding hands until the music stops and you dance with whoever's in front of you, and then with the one you've been thinking about, in your circle of friends, when you dance together, the cornmeal sliding beneath your feet, let go, take a chance, nuzzle in, what can you lose but screaming nights of wind and cold sheets and only the dog to put your arms around.

And in the crowded hall of the Legion, where we dance to Blue Diamond, beneath the blue and cream lattice ceiling, and Albert reaches up for a Valentine balloon for every woman in the room, where everyone dances with each other, and sometimes women dance with women, then put your arms around this man you've been thinking of, weren't ready for until now, and sway tighter and longer. And when he says, after a night of dancing and laughing with Glen who fills up the oil tank, and Linda and Linda the postmistresses, and

Georgie and Cecil and Edwina and Andy and Chris, when he tells you with his fisherman's hands, gentle and strong, just at the waist, that he wants you, too, and looks at you steady and says would you come down home with me tonight, say yes and make your exit. You can always try to get back on course if it's a wrong one.

And together you can steer yourselves through suicidal February with his home-made bread and rappie pie and your music and the lobster he brings in from the boat and making love a hundred times because it's cold and your skin has been covered so long and the pipes broke and brought you all a little closer, so take it as a gift and see survival gear when it looks at you and says let's ward off the cold.

✦

Letters home

Dear Caroline, Dear Bonnie, Dear Corky, Dear Bernie and Sab,

The people do not argue here, not as a form of conversation. They argue at home, they argue with their children, with husbands and wives. But they do not wrangle as a form of discourse.

I said one day to my friend, People don't argue here and he agreed with me. No, I mean, you don't argue. And he wouldn't take me up on it.

If a person says the day is dirty, the next one doesn't say well, it's not nearly as bad as the day I got caught out alone in the bay. Now that was windy.

No, they say, if you say, it's a dirty day, they say, dirty, it's dirty all right. And then they might volunteer a story that included you, like the time you both got caught out together, and then together you build the tale.

Do you see what I mean?

At home in B.C. I mostly remember arguing. Fighting over details like chickens grabbing a trapped mouse. Rip. Tear.

The story ends up tattered.

DEAR FRIENDS THAT I LOVE back home who I miss and sometimes cry for,

I have not been homesick. I have not missed the closed-in sky. But today someone loved me, and I wailed. I knelt on the floor and I wailed. I called your name over and over, I could not find my breath, I braced myself on the floor, on my knees, on all fours, and I could see the oak beneath my hands, and my stomach lurched like a dog throwing up stolen food, convulsed like birth, and I cried for you, as if calling your name would mean you were alive, bring you back, and I was afraid to find out by lifting the receiver, as if my loneliness, my loss of you, would make it real.

And my friend said, you call them, you call home and you find out everything that is happening and you have a long yarn and you'll feel better. No, I said, I won't. I can't. I can't know anything. Not for a while.

We don't have a family in B.C., but sometimes the family we make is so strong, the bonds so tight, the hurts so bitter and the love so fierce, that sometimes we have to leave.

Maybe we don't even know how to be a family yet, we've only been doing it for 20 years. Don't get the ebb and flow yet, the times to back off, the times to close the door, the times to say this is a social event, a time for pictures and stories. And hush, hush, my dear ones.

✦

I'd like to give you the weather network for your birthday

I FEEL YOU HERE BESIDE ME on this trip. Sometimes.
You are in my dreams. You are dying. You are com-
manding. You are comforting, and what I know now,
you figured out long ago. I need to leave you behind,
and in my dreams you have died and then there you are
again huddled in your chair.

I would like to give you the weather network for
your birthday, a gift of this trip, something we don't
have back home.

The perfect gift for a prairie girl, packaged features
on tornadoes, droughts, grasshoppers, icy highways
and snow shovelled overhead.

I would like you to see and dream about the ocean,
the ferries lifting and crashing in the salt, laughter and
fear. I'd like to give you the daily road report, once an
hour, so you could plan, and watch across the country.

The small piles of accidents, like laundry heaped
on the highways, El Niño, hurricanes, snowstorms, the
three-day outlook, so you could know, judge, take a
calculated risk after watching the rebroadcast hour
after hour. Or you could say stop, say not today, today
is too dangerous, I am not ready.

Today I will stay in my housecoat, pull my bones

beneath me, read and not leave this spot until the night pulls down over the mountains. Or watch the weather network, hour after hour, keeping track of upheaval everywhere.

✦

If I had a baby,
I'd name her Edwina, or Caroline

STAUNCH AND FUNNY, both of them, sturdy and sexy, that's how I want my girl to be. The kind of heart that has borne and lost babies and keeps on fighting and loving. Breasts or hips too large or small, bound them into the world, firm women, laughter as large as buttocks lifted in aerobics, all women, grunting, whining, thrusting, sniggering, clapping and collapsing when a rumpled piece of fabric softener drifts down to the floor from the armpit of a newly laundered t-shirt. Rural women horsing around in their firehalls.

Two rural women, Caroline from the Peace River a million miles back in B.C., Edwina of this island. Caroline with her blonde pony's mane and Edwina with her black, with rural plain talk for haemorrhoids or haemorrhage, kicked him in the nuts or cried my guts out for her, and they did. Freckled, swimmers, raised in the water, skaters raised on the ice, firewood to make, snow and horses in winter, grass fires to tend and calves to pull in spring, would chase a man cross country if he was the right one, and they did. Saw him at the gas station, the Fish and Game dance, and that was it.

Would hold you in the night, or day, gather you up,

not afraid of women, the kind of woman you could murmur to.

I want my girl to be named Caroline, or Edwina.

✦

Loaves and fishes

DANIEL HAS REMOVED his pajama bottoms and, bare-bummed, pulls on Edwina's brown, pink and blue knit aerobics leggings over his firm boy thighs. She laughs and cuddles him to her, content for the night as the men bicker over their best bread recipes.

Lloyd and Cecil both baked today, a day off fishing, time to experiment with the new islands cookbook, *From Hash to Haddock*, its pale green cover floury on their counters, as the muscles that pull up lobster traps knead the bread, the tattoos from the Lunenburg exhibition 20 years ago pulling and knotting with the dough. A loaf bare in his broad hand, Lloyd sneaks up behind Cecil, flourishes it for his brother's approval. Try this, he says.

Parker smiles and inspects the bread of the two younger men.

He is talking about flour barrels, how in the war the family survived with the big bins of flour — white flour it was, too. Can't starve a fishing village — fish, canned milk, and flour. What happened to those barrels? Oh, probably threw 'em away, didn't know they'd be valuable now.

Fishing stories mix with recipes from the old sailing

ships, and there's scallops and lobster and clam chowders, mussels orange and female and bursting, cloud biscuits, snails, haddock and cod.

✦

Chainsaw

WE'RE SITTING IN THE LIVING ROOM, telling stories, the first time since the water pipe broke and ruined the ceiling and floor. Cecil and Edwina, who discovered the mess, Andy and Chris and me.

It's blustery out there by the Bay of Fundy, and we're enjoying the new fireplace, the warmth of the flames, before we head out to the dance at the Legion. I had to borrow Cecil's chainsaw to buck up the firewood because my brother's is a borrowed Craftsman someone bought for $25 at a rummage sale and even that was robbery.

Cecil's is a real chainsaw, even if it is a Pioneer. It's loud and fast, sharp and heavy, spits out wood chips in big chunks, the sign of sharpness, no sawdust filling your nose. The smell of chain oil and mixed gas. The smell of getting things done.

Except of course we're talking about chainsaws, and anyone with a whit of grace knows some rules about chainsaws.

Andy and Cecil recall the time they were working on the new septic, and Cecil was over with the saw, bragging it up, like how it always started, and how he kept two saws in good working condition, and sharp and such. And how some people didn't maintain their equipment. And so there he was pulling the cord to start up the saw to cut up the old ties for the septic cover, but he'd bragged up that saw so much of course it wouldn't start. And he pulled and he pulled, and they fetched screwdrivers from Andy's shop and Cecil's barn, and they adjusted the high jet and the low jet, and they cleaned filters and may have even gone so far as to change the gas.

It reminded Cecil of that other time he bought a used saw at the chainsaw place near Digby, and when he got it home of course it wouldn't work. It wouldn't and it wouldn't, nothing you could do with the damn thing. So he phones the guy back at the store and the guy says I'll give you $75 for it but you'd probably get more satisfaction if you beat it to death in your driveway. So that's what Cecil did, drove over it a couple times. And as anyone knows who's ever handled a chainsaw, that would be a lot of satisfaction.

Like back home in B.C., there's the logger sports competition in Slocan City, and one of the best ones I like, even more than the derring-do of the log burling in the water, the balancing act and the pirouettes, is the chainsaw-throwing contest. Where you see these loggers, and you imagine they're out there in the bush, where the flies are at them, or the mosquitoes, or the bills to pay, or maybe it's just an absolutely fine day, the kind of day you can make up for the days of lousy spindly wood, and get some nice timber, and the saw won't start. Like sometimes all you need is to concede, and this is where grace comes in, just pass the saw to someone else who will do the exact same thing you were doing, and the saw will start.

It's a kind of test, like some days you can laugh at things and take them in stride, and say, here, you give it a go, and when someone else starts it for you, you laugh, get back to work, and you know some day you'll do the same for them.

But then there's the days when that's not how you are. There are days when you must fix it yourself because pride makes you. There are the days you say I will do this by my goddamn self, and when I personally am that ornery, I will not ask a goddamn man for help, even though the next day I might if I needed it and that person had the skill, and if they were gracious about it.

Now this is what it's like with chainsaws. There are days you'd rather beat them to death and walk off the mountain smiling, than to hand it to someone else for help. That's why the chainsaw-throwing contest is my favourite. They pull and they pull and the saw just goes *ruh-ruh* and sometimes you'll hear the clacking as the cord whips back into the casing on its roulette wheel, and you can feel how that handle whips back into the part between your thumb and your first finger, and how sometimes you'll yank that cord so often your hand gets bruised-up and red and stiff.

If you're in the contest, you throw it, make that baby

sail as far as it will go, not like a discus, but a shove, just push that thing as far from you as you can, cause it's you or it, and on some days you gotta win, somehow.

So it's easy to see how Cecil, I can imagine him now, streak of grease across his face, curls smashed down under a hat, Jesus Edwina I'm trying to fix the saw, how he must have felt when that time at the septic, after Andy'd gone off to borrow another saw from a neighbour, after he'd had the frigging thing in pieces on the ground, and damn near lost a part or two down the septic, how he must have felt when my brother looked at Cecil, and then at the saw and then back at Cecil again, and said, don't you have to turn on the switch?

✦

This dog a Newfoundland?

EVEN IN A BLIZZARD people went visiting, Parker says, sitting on the daybed next to the scanner that barks out the English and French gossip amongst the fishing fleet. This dog a Newfoundland? he asks while petting Connor who is in full lean against him.

We'd go round from house to house playing cards, sometimes all night if the weather was bad and no one could go fishing. Or we'd get all the kids in the neighbourhood doing the limbo. Lloyd was the one who could limbo lowest. His back would be almost on the floor.

Or we'd put a pin on the floor, then bend down from the waist and pick it up in our mouths. You can't put your hands on the floor. Try it. You gotta put your legs out and keep them straight. See? Don't fall over. Legs get some strained, don't they?

I take that one home and try it out on Lloyd and Krystal and her cousin Kristie. You do it like this, I said, and pulled my leg muscle right through into the next month.

✦

Men must work and women must weep

DON'T TURN HIM INTO A SISSY, he said, this old beaten man who'd fished the east coast and the west, when times were hard, try another coast, keep working, keep fishing, travel long and hard, like his face, rolling a cigarette and squinting through the smoke. Don't let your boys be sissies, he said, men don't cry.

But there was that time when three men sat together, each, one after the other, lost a child, at the age of 19 months, 22 months, 24 months. In a living room they sat, just sat, holding each other, crying over the latest loss. Who else could know, who else could understand.

Men don't cry, he said.

Except that time down at Beautiful Cove, when two men sat in a truck, one weeping for what he'd lost, what he had to do, quit drinking, put his life in order, and he did, after another man listened and let him cry long and hard.

Men can't be sissies, he said, they don't cry, he said.

Except for the time when with the women, they helped bring a doctor back to the island, to bring safety here where the tides are highest, the storms the strongest, and the hospital the furthest, and when they found the doctor they couldn't talk, none of them, the doctor, all of them, they started crying before they started laughing.

Don't cry, he said, *except when your child comes to your arms and asks, what did I do wrong daddy, why aren't we a family anymore?*

Don't cry, he said, you can't be a sissy, you have to be strong in these winds, these tides, these dangers. Leave it to the women to do the crying.

✦

Quilt of fish

YOU COULD SEE THE FISH COMING, Parker says, coming just the same as waving a quilt, and he waves his arms in billows, and in the undulations I can see the water and the movement of the fish, as if he were waving a quilt in the wind. Pollock as far as you could see, and the gulls followed them, he says. My soul, what fun.

This is Parker: twisting together the monogrammed pool cue, PMT, Parker Matthew Thurber. This is Parker, caring for his Anna, whirling Cecil's lobster boat in the shallow waters by the rip, knows every rock, could take you so near you could step out onto the land. This is Parker: cribbage whiz, Parker pointing out shipwrecks, Parker outwitting the fisheries officer, Parker the politician, steering himself through a cantankerous ratepayers' meeting. This is Parker, too, crying on the phone from the hospital, lonely, scared, there's too much left to do, help Edwina, never missed a lobster supper at the firehall, watch more children get big, find that notebook, where is it, full of the important papers, somewhere in the house.

Parker twists the pool cue together in a gentle but firm grip, looks up at Edwina who's sighting down the line of a #17.

Ready Parker? she asks, purple oversized t-shirt, purple International Women's Day earrings, yellow, purple and hot pink swirls on skin-tight pedal-pushers she just bought at the Evangeline Mall in Digby, $8 on sale. She's two months pregnant. She nurses a 7-Up while Parker orders his usual, vodka and water.

The other day Parker walked into Edwina's and found her crying — sitting there over all her letters of resignation, from the village commission, cemetery committee, harbour authority, the committee trying to bring a doctor back to the island. She can't do it any more, not without more support, not with two boys climbing over everything, taking in more kids to help the family income, a baby on the way, dealing with sick and dying relatives.

Parker puts his arms around Edwina, says I love you like a daughter, I am so proud of you, and decides then and there he'll go back into politics to help her out.

This is Parker, who is in all the stories, the time he and Edwina killed the roosters, the time the first union was organized long ago, his days on the school board, his love for Anna.

I want to know him, sense my own urgency in this, and he tells me stories by his window looking over the cove, amidst the shelves of old crockery the antique collectors come to scavenge, or on the nights we play crib, at his home or in the hospital. Parker is in the stories, he is of the stories, he is the storyteller.

This is Parker, selling the boat, baking the bread, milking cows and tending chickens, making home with Anna and the three girls.

I don't like this where the men go off and get drunk and leave the women to do all the work, he says. Marriage is 50/50.

When Anna was 32 she got polio. I sold the boat. She was named *Margaret Elaine* after our daughter. She was an all-round boat, 40 feet long and 14 feet wide, not just for lobster, and I sold her after having her six months.

We got 75 hens and three cows, and we took in paying house-guests, people on holidays. Anna got well enough to walk, but the last ten years she went downhill. A year after she got polio, they came out with insurance against it, but I couldn't get it for the kids because she already had polio.

She hated this, he says, wrestling with the shower-chair stored in the upstairs closet. One day someone'll have to put me in it, Parker says.

The entire upstairs is spare bedrooms for when the children and grandchildren come home.

When he tells me there was no medicare then for

their family, that the bill for the spinal puncture was $6,000, that the roads weren't paved and Halifax a day away, I remember again how us kids were raised with stories of Stanley Knowles in mum's Winnipeg home. I thought, this is what they were doing, making it so Parker and Anna wouldn't have to live this way. All those little meetings in living rooms. How my mother, many years later, said if you want to talk to Stanley Knowles, you call him, because there won't always be time, and so I did.

Parker tells me the Conservative MP, George Nowlin, simply took the bill from him and said, you're not paying this. Since then, Parker has worked to get a nurse's station on the island, and to bring a doctor back to the islands.

Where do I get my social convictions? I got asked that before. What makes you tick, this man asked me, someone from the social council or something. I said, now that's a stupid question. You do it because you enjoy it. We got raised like that, from the time we were 12; our father taught us to help people, and not for money. We carried people's coal and kindling. It was our duty, and we got to enjoy it.

Then one night, in the hospital, he says, when Anna was 67, I had to ask her twice to kiss me. I never had to do that before. She died that night.

But my god we had some fun, he says, stroking Connor, who leans against him. This dog of yours a Newfoundland?

77

This is Parker, who won't live anywhere else.

Parker's friend Melda has got her cancer back again. She's had a stroke and she doesn't recognize anyone.

My god it's hard to believe just a few weeks ago we were playing cards. I was so lonely last night, looking out and seeing there is no light at Melda's. There won't be a light on again. That light won't go on again.

Melda and I went to a seniors mixer on the French Shore last month, he says. It's to get the cultures mixing. We go there and play cards, and we laugh, and we listen to music, that fellow there who used to play with the ClareTones, my word he can play. And we eat Rappie pie. I didn't think I liked it and who was the first one up for seconds.

And we're driving home down the neck, and I think, why would anyone want to live anywhere else but Freeport. Other places there is nothing to see but cars on the road, maybe some trees. But when you drive over Crocker's Hill and see the lights of the village reflecting on the water, and where a senior has never been hurt at night, not like the city where you can't go for a walk without carrying a gun on your hip, and I can talk to the kids and even the wild ones would never think of hurting me. No, baby, I'm staying right here until the last shot is fired. They ain't taking me no-where.

✦

The gulls sing a different song in spring

KRYSTAL'S RAPPING AND JIVING. She's 13, grade six, 4'9", size five, a live wire, a Nova Scotia accent as thick as the chowder her Dad makes from the scallops off his dragger.

Da-ad, can I fish the dragger when I'm older, she says the day they take it to the shipyard over in Meteghan down the French shore. She squirms in through the side window into the wheelhouse. Lots of women do, Lloyd says, at the wheel, waiting to move the *Krystal Anne*, named after Krystal and her mother, through the ice and up onto the slip for the annual government inspection.

She's digging for tapes, but the tape deck's long gone. She's into every cupboard. After you get off the dragger, you roll with the water back on the land, she says.

At the Islands Consolidated School variety night, three girls set their baseball caps backward, tuck in their hair, wear outlandish oversized sunglasses and giant floppy day-glo runners. The two boys wear dresses, and they all dance up on the stage. Strobe lights flickering, Krystal is the smallest and the fastest and she could hop and wiggle for hours.

Sometimes Krystal wishes she had a sister. There was another baby girl, but she died on a spring day long before Krystal was born, strangled in the backyard fence her Dad built, her brothers too big to wiggle into it but she did. Krystal and her Dad stop by Monique's grave after buying Rappie pie at Pointe-de-L'Église — Church Point — across from the huge wooden Catholic church, they lean together, balancing the pan of steaming chicken and potatoes between them, talking about Monique as if Krystal knew her.

Krystal marches into her aunt Edwina's house, slaps her Regal catalogue onto the table, starts her sales pitch. She's got $600 squirrelled away and wants more. One day she'll use it to buy a stereo, the next day it's for college, another day for a shopping trip to Halifax, she's heard there's some malls down there.

In the Yarmouth mall, she sees the boy she likes, and tracks him through notions, where he's following his mother.

I'm never getting married, Dad, she says as she writes this boy's name in her diary 20 times, and her Dad sits mending the bedding for the dragger.

She knows both worlds, this Krystal with two earrings in each lobe. The wheelhouse and the home, the galley and the kitchen, rolling on the water, rocking on the land.

Da-ad, do you have any money, 'cause I'm gonna take the babysitting course where they teach you what to do if a kid's choking.

Da-ad, will you teach me to drive the truck?
Da-ad, I'm taking the dog for a walk!
Da-ad, can I have a sip of beer?
Da-ad, will you buy me the teen pack at Shopper's?
Her white leggings, scuffed white boots, coat to her knees, dark curls long and blowing back in the Atlantic wind, even the mousse and gel won't keep them down.

She squirms in through the dragger's window, Krystal Crocker, crystal and crockery salvaged from the shipwrecks of these waters, galley and kitchen, the surviving treasure of the Atlantic.

The gulls sing a different song in spring, her Dad said.

✦

Recipe for a compost heap

ONE PART RABBIT PELLETS, one part chicken, in the
yard where Helen Moore asks if I've been to the dance,
if we're living together, but she's talking so fast, her
accent so strong, that — embarrassed — I cannot understand, and thinking I must be deaf, stupid and rude, she
calls louder and again, Did we go to the dance? Are you
living with him? And smiles.

We fill a fish tote with rabbit shit, and the chickens
red and black, with just one Leghorn, white, peck
around the red back buildings, while the rabbit hound
on its chain and the Chesapeake Bay Retriever or is it
a chocolate lab, pause on their runs, and the third dog,
the grey-muzzled lab, the family pet, watches as the
blue, red and yellow whirligigs twirl on the front lawn.

Three totes rockweed from Beautiful Cove, with
the sand fleas hopping out from steaming scoops, like
hot manure, even in the Atlantic spray in May, the truck
parked down as far on the rocks as we dare.

One plastic bucket pollock heads and backbones,
from way down on the boat below the wharf where
Rawleigh Bates looks up from Tony Thurber's boat
and Richard Titus turns his head up too while I lower
the bucket. Rawleigh and Richard who walk together

everywhere, around the village every day, Rawleigh
who used to dig the graves, always looking down at the
road, old coveralls, Richard big with swinging arms,
wave to you every day, meet you and sit awhile near
Cow Ledge, hands shoved in their pockets as they
trudge along.

One bucket fish meal from the reduction plant at
Mink Cove, where D.B. Kenney plants truck their
offal; pollock, cod and halibut, now reduced to ferti-
lizer for the gardens overlooking the ocean.

Three parts grass clippings, raked up in handfuls
from the long spots at Edwina's and Cecil's below
where the dogs are tied on runs, and the grass grown in
dark-green clumps. Dried old manure from the coop
they brought over on the back of Vernon and Jackie's
truck, the old henhouse moved from one neighbour to
the next as they try out chickens once again.

One bag lobster shells, from the Easter feast with
Parker, arriving precisely at five, in his three-piece
going-out-places suit, when I forgot that old people
don't arrive fashionably late but come prepared for
hours and hours of stories and company and no time
to lose. And he moves to the map of shipwrecks, some
he's seen, the three-masted schooner that went down
past Dartmouth Point, and he looks at the old village
map, can name every merchant, every captain, can
trace their children to the ones he knows now from the
day the village showed up to clean up the playground.
The lobster shells, tough and orange and sharp, grow

moist and hot in the compost, the orange fading, shell softening, with fishbone and seaweed, grass and manure, until they will crumble like fired and steaming earth.

✦

Ranch romance

On the lobster boat I can see him smiling. The boat twists and charges like a barrel racer, start stop swirl near the buoy, water billowing around us like the dirt from a pony's hooves.

Lloyd sits on the curb boards, knowing his brother's antics without watching him in the wheelhouse. Lloyd is looking out on their ocean, the Bay of Fundy he could never leave. He grabs the gaff, the pole with the hook on the end, the kind you see even on inland ferries like ours back in B.C., for pulling up whatever is overboard.

He hooks the buoy, hauls it up, slips the rope onto the winch, hauling 45 fathoms, the traps up from the bottom, throws me the buoy to dunk into the bleach water to kill a year's worth of algae, at the stern, bob the buoy with the end of a broom, flat and stubby, like the kind they use now in curling, no more graceful swish.

Dunk, dunk, dunk, the bleach spray slaps up to lighten my hair, my old sweatshirt, leaking in through the collar of my yellow raingear. I can see Cecil and Lloyd hauling the traps, they'll do 375 today — about 60 pounds each empty, just with the cement slab that keeps it on bottom.

It's too cold, the lobster aren't moving, huddled in
their shells down in the dark, they don't even want to go
out to eat the bait. Only the crabs are scuttling, the
useless crabs, no market for this kind, with legs and legs
and legs clutching the sides of the wire traps — maybe
20 crabs in a trap — 160 legs grabbing hold, don't want
to be shook out into the ocean. These brothers have to
flip the cages over, a 60-pound bench press, lift the cage
again and again, crack it down on the side of the boat,
loosen the crabs to make them fall, grab them with stiff
gloves that will only get warm when held against the
exhaust pipes wrapped in asbestos lagging that looks
like burlap, the smell of stinking bait herring and
orange rubber gloves steaming against the pipes. In the
first hours, they smash crabs against the curb boards,
crab legs crashed in anger, bodies broken to filter to the
lobster below. Crabs thrown into the vat of bleach,
though I fish them out with my stubby broom and flip
them into the salt water to infest another trap.

After the first hour, at another string of buoys, they
find a lobster every fourth trap, not the three or four
they get per trap when the prices are low. Sure the price
went up to $10 a pound when the lobster stayed put and
wouldn't go near a trap, and water froze on the deck,
and the groaners were never silent and the snow lashed.
Now the price is down to $6.50 and plummeting as fast
as the traps.

It's the first day out in two weeks, and they'll bring
in 100 pounds of lobster. When the weather warms

and it's decent to work, then lobster will be down to $3 or less again, like before the strike.

But at least there's a lobster now and then, and as the shoulders and backs warm in the constant work, the crabs are simply tipped overboard, the anger a waste. Some boats never let a crab go alive, bury them all in a dump site, smash them.

Cecil's pouring coffee from the tall green thermos, instant made at 5:30 this morning, and untwists the tie on the Ben's white bread sandwich bag. The cheez whiz tastes soothing; liver paté is fine with a beer after work, but it's nauseating here in the stench of bait and steaming pipes and chlorine. Cheez whiz. Cheese paté, we call it. I sit in the moulded plastic white garden chair in the corner across the engine platform, four cylinder Detroit Diesel, eating cheez whiz, covered in chlorine and salt water, and ask Cecil if he can make the boat buck faster.

His boat's called the *Kristie and Shannon*, not his own naming. It came with the boat. Most boats are named after family, an honour to the name.

Georgie's finally getting a new boat. Friends and family took his old one out, it was rotten and dangerous, and burned it in the water off Freeport. Not without his permission, but fairly much at their insistence. And now Georgie's grabbing arms at the Legion, he can't stand not fishing, he says. The waiting's gonna kill him, and he squeezes harder. You're a wonderful woman,

87

and you got a fine man, he says. I'm telling ya, he's a good man. He's had a hard life, and he's fished hard, and he studied hard to bring himself up, and I'm telling ya, he loves ya. You're a good woman. By the christ I want that boat and I don't know what to do with myself. I've always fished. I love it. I love fishing. I love fishing, don't I, Lloyd? Isn't that true, Cecil? I love fishing. Fished all my life, haven't I? You know what I'm calling her? I'm calling her *Georgie Porgie*, that's true.

Georgie Porgie, that's what they called me all my life and that's the name I'm giving her. Never got no education, but I fished hard and I love it, I tell you I love it. Georgie Porgie, puddin'n'pie. Edwina helped me fill out the forms. We had to give three names, in case one was already taken, so we put down *Georgie Porgie*, *Georgie Porgie II* and *Georgie Porgie III*. You ever hear tell of that name before? No, I ain't seen no boat named *Georgie Porgie* before. I'm telling ya, I'm gonna love fishing that boat.

Out across the way, I can see some other fishermen smashing crabs. Everyone waves, curious about the yellow-hooded stranger on the *Kristie and Shannon*, but are friendly anyway. At home in B.C., if I'm mad at someone, I stop waving. One time it had been so long that I forgot why I was mad, had to ask a friend if they remembered. On these boats, on these roads, grudges are a luxury.

On another boat, there's a woman fishing. She

worked the post office before, but now she's starting on
the boats, and her husband is proud. So is she. They've
come after us for some fresh bait from the nets dropped
in Beautiful Cove. There's an overstuffed chair, domestic, in the corner of the wheelhouse, for the moments of nausea, or fatigue, have to sit a minute, when
you're not out slitting fish bellies, scrubbing the white
meat with the stiff brush dipped in salt water, preparing
the bodies for the heavy salt vats or fresh fish sales,
removing every mark of blood, the little pockets where
the fins grow from the inside. Cheryl Guier's smiling.
It's good out here. Later in the Legion, Anne Crocker's
been out fishing, too. She's small, Krystal her daughter
is so like her. I am beginning to see the women who fish.
Fisherwomen.

Fantasy: one day Edwina will tell Cecil you take the
kids, we're going fishing. And Krystal, Lloyd's daughter, Edwina's niece, will come with us, and Edwina will
take the wheel of the *Kristie and Shannon,* open the
window before her, spray making her laugh, then settle
in for some hard fishing. She squints her eyes to the
spray, revs up the engine, and we laugh as we pass
another boat where the women look up from their lines
and wave.

And at day's end, backs aching, feet numb, we'll
pull up to the wharf, wave at old Keith Titus up above
on his motor scooter with the big plastic milk crate on
the back, and Parker up there too, calling down a

greeting, smiling, remembering his own days like this, and we'll jump from boat to boat, throwing the ropes up to Keith and Parker to loop over the logs heads or lasso the metal cleats. And the big rubber balloons, the bladder balls, will keep the *Kristie and Shannon* from rocking too sharply against her neighbour. The fish we haven't had time to clean coming in, we'll clean there at the wharf, greeting the others as they steam in.

Then we'll go home, say hi to the kids, and head to the Legion for a beer.

◆

We are not sentimental, because this is food

WE WILL BE LIKE THE BEARS. We will rip the heads from our prey. Rip open their hot intestines, using our bare hands. Flesh to flesh. What we do not eat we leave as carrion.

Like Caroline, when the car hit the fool hen, she jumped from the van, it still rumbling, five swift steps to the bird, a twist of the neck. Supper.

On the boat, there is no way to stun the fish — it only hurts them. Better to be quick, with the knife, gulls waiting alongside, quickly, head laid back, thumb holding back the jaw, slit the throat, through the artery, the cut behind the gills, then slit the belly, two cuts up to the back of the head, push the head back down against the edge of the slaughter box, press down hard, break it off leaving the V of meat at the back, throw the head to the gulls, they dodge and feint, leave it to sink, waiting for intestines. The head, now carrion for scavengers, lobster and crab. Slip out the guts, the gulls and haglins flap up from the water, dive from where they hover, the haglin swimming down below the surface, diving like the fish can never do again, flying below the water. The fish is on ice before it has stopped moving.

We are the bear, our claw the knife, the strength in

91

the arms, the back and neck, pivoting on strong legs.
We are not sentimental, because this is food. Instead,
we are fast.

In Creston, back in B.C., the apples pulled me
over, a souvenir of home to take to friends
across the country, and besides, Truscott, the
name says on the fruitstand. Are these the
farmers who broke ranks with their party to
support ours, or is this the brother, the local
Socred party president. I can't resist the last
connection with home and politics before leaving the mountains. And besides, how can I
drive past in the sun, a day saying do not ignore
one chance of me. Later I see the coyote on the
road, too, slow down in snow in the Crowsnest,
and we look into each other's eyes, we nod and
keep on our ways as the dog sleeps in the back.
Yellow apples, like yellow eyes, pulled me in,
and the farmer is the Socred, not his rebel
brother, but it's a sunny day after the election,
and in the middle of his pumpkins and apples,
I haul out pictures of the campaign, taken in his
town, taken on the farms, on the streets, farmers pulling wagons of apples and wearing our
party's buttons. He laughs, and I like leaving
B.C. better with his smile upon me.

I am peeling Annapolis apples in the kitchen on the

Bay of Fundy, listening to the farm rallies on Parliament Hill. 40,000 farmers in Ottawa. 1,500 in Halifax, and Fredericton, they are out in Winnipeg and Victoria. It is Feb. 21st, they are out in the cold, used to it this time of year, we've seen them a hundred times in the stories about Saskatchewan, their breath frosty in the air next to the flank of a scruffy-haired range cow. They've come on tractors and planes, ferries, and a few found the train, to say — keep cheap imports out of the country. It means the survival of our farms. Our culture. Our country.

A farmer from Nova Scotia speaks first. Later he will run for the province's Liberal leadership, but they never can scrape enough chicken dung off his boots to win the city vote. The farmers are saying you let them dump cheap American food here and you'll wreck our farms. The woman from the Consumers Association of Canada tells me on the radio in the kitchen on the Bay of Fundy where I am peeling Annapolis apples, she says let's have megafarms. Import it all from the States. More efficient, cheaper. Better for the consumer. I yell at her, and cheer for the farmers.

I think of my trip, of Grazyna's pickles, cucumbers grown in the broad fields of Southern Alberta, the apples from Creston, root crops stored and saved for winter, pumpkins in the sun at the fruitstand, laughing and pictures, lobster and scallops in the Bay of Fundy, the jam my friend is making in her kitchen near Sudbury as she stirs and talks, the chickens in my freezer we killed before the election, the sunflowers of Saskatchewan that remind me of the Doukhobors back home who once lived on these prairies. Each piece of food can tell its own story, if we were there to make the story with it.

The woman from the consumers' association doesn't care about stories. She doesn't care if megafarms in the U.S. mean death, if it's a fast one or a slow one. We cannot be sentimental, because this is food.

✦

S U R V I V A L   G E A R

Can't resist fish cakes

YOU'D THINK YOU WERE BORN a hundred years ago,
the way you put the molasses to those fish cakes, Parker
says. Belong in another century, he says.

He's been out of the hospital a week now, after a
month of pneumonia, and he's been out visiting most
nights. Tonight he's dropped by to pick up some fresh
haddock Lloyd's brought him from the boat. He's
spent the afternoon with Edwina and the kids.

He's eaten supper but can't resist fish cakes, salt
cod from the vats in the fish shed, rinsed again and
again, then cooked and mashed with potatoes, and
fried in the pan, the texture of the fish still firm.

The talk always turns to fishing, and we turn down
the TV, settle onto the couches, and Lloyd hauls out
the fish book with its photos and drawings in the kind
of detail some books give on birds. They sit together,
paging through pictures of blister-back pollock, redfish,
haddock, cod and lobster. My god we had some fun,
Parker says.

He leans into the story. People had to feed their
families, he says. In those days when we'd fish lobster,
the full-sized ones we had to sell. But we'd bring some
undersized ones home, or cook one up for our dinner

95

on board. The fisheries inspectors wouldn't stand for that. One feller, he sees the fisheries coming after him just as he's finishing his dinner, so he dumps the shells overboard. But they're bright orange, and they float, and they left a trail right to him.

One time I see the fisheries, and my Jesus, they're coming after me, and I can't hide a kettle of steaming lobster. I'd been hauling traps, so I got one up fast, dumped the whole steaming pot into it, threw it overboard and took off for my next string of markers. When I looked back I could see that steam rising off the water as the trap settled down. I went back later and hauled it up, and those lobster were done to perfection. Cooled down perfectly.

People have to feed themselves and their families, he says. But greed and plunder he can't tolerate, not from anyone, not from insiders or out. And he tells about the time he found an American boat fishing with drift nets near Beatson's buoy. Those nets that fish forever, he says, they kill everything, the lobster and the gulls, the dolphins and the fish. Those nets drift in the ocean and kill and kill. I went out there in my boat, he says. I balled up their net, anchors and all, so it could never fish or drift again.

It's been nine years since I fished, he says. I'd go out there again in a minute if I could.

A week ago from the hospital Parker asked me to look out the window and tell him what the ocean was doing. It's cold and there's mist, I told him.

SURVIVAL GEAR

That old ocean's steaming, Parker said. It hasn't
seen the sun for so long it don't know what to do.

✦

Bragging you up

The Potato
There are girls who can speak
Both Latin and Greek
And quote Aristotle and Plato
But who can compare
Be she ever so fair
To the girl who can cook a potato?
  From Hash to Haddock
  Heirloom Recipes of Westport, Nova Scotia

He's been working all day, every day, scrubbing down
the scallop dragger, travelling each day across the Petite
Passage ferry, up to the Middle Cross road, then down
the French Shore to Meteghan to A.F. Theriault's boat
shop — putting the dragger on the slip, it's called. And
while the workmen, Acadian all, dressed in winter gear
and quilted hats with ear flaps and strings hanging down
from the caps, work over the boat in the cold so brittle
and swept off St. Mary's Bay, inside the boat he and
Greg work too.

They scrub with bristle pads and Pine Sol, they
scrub each cupboard, every bunk, the dollar-sized welt

on his hand from the day he burned it on my oven broiler becomes a sweating ooze from the disinfectants and the new verathane, the scrubbing of the oil stove in the galley, the dust and grunge.

But I am not thinking of this when I say, you were telling your friend about the meals I cook for you? That is what you have to say about me?

You don't know how much it means to have a hot meal after those days, he said. I tell Greg while we work in that dirt and it makes his mouth water — how you made me scallops in wine, or garlic chicken, or the lasagna.

The little woman, eh? is my reply, the hairs raising on my back, the acid eating at my stomach.

He turns from me, hurt, not understanding, honest in his praise.

Did you tell him how I handle a chainsaw, how I split wood? I ask, knowing how dumb this sounds even as I spit it out. I have rarely praised anyone to a third party for how well they split wood.

But it's my only response. Someone praises my cooking they better balance it with something. And even though I know this is ridiculous, that my come-back is laughable even to me, I am still rankled. In this village I do not want to be seen as his girlfriend or my brother's sister, although of course that is unavoidable since I am the new person and these links will be made.

So any rebuttal, even a poor one, seems necessary.

Do you think I'm going to say to Greg, yes, she

really is something, you should see her split that wood.
No, I tell him that I love you, that you have been here
for me when I come home cold and wet and frozen. I
tell him about your opinions and your points of view.
Your outlook on things. That is what matters.

And I am ashamed. How many nights when I have
worked late, been away, has he held dinner for me, fed
the kids early and then waited for me, to heat up
chowder he made from the scallops and lobster he's
caught. How is it I can forget he called me and invited
me for the Rappie pie he made. The individual por-
tions he wraps and freezes, so the kids can get their own
suppers. How I tell my friends back home about the
wonderful bread he bakes.

But still.

To praise a man for his cooking is to say, this is a
different kind of man. This man does not leave the job
to the woman. To say a man can cook, and likes to
cook, means he has paid attention.

Even if he cooks, everyone always knows that what
he is is of the earth, the ocean, the world.

For a woman to make a hot meal for a man, and be
there waiting, means something different. Like the day
I visited Edwina and found that in each of our houses
we were baking lemon chicken for supper for the
brothers who were both out fishing. Oh dear, I said.
Isn't this domestic?

I try to explain, feeling my way through his hurt and
my bristling and my shame.

And in the end he says, I know what you mean. You want to be known for yourself.

But I still think you're a good cook.

✦

Contrary-minded

I LIKE THIS EXPRESSION, contrary-minded. It comes up at the local ratepayers meeting. There's no attempt at consensus, or sitting on your opinion for the sake of some kind of smothered peace.

All those in favour? All those contrary-minded? and all the grumpy people get to join together and declare their contrariness. Hrmphh. We're the cranky people and outright up front you should know we don't like this thing and you'll hear about it for a few days, too. At the Legion, or at the post office or the grocery or the seniors' drop-in. Right out front. The grumpy people.

My dog peed on your rhubarb? You and everyone in town will talk about it at the ratepayers meeting. Hrmphh. Someone's got boards stacked in their yard or hasn't mowed recently? They'll hear about that, too.

And here they are arguing about the electric rates at the community hall, and who left on the heater anyway, and I'm taken back home to B.C., the community hall and who pays what portion of the bill, how do the users divvy it up, and our meeting is informal, sitting around a table, trying to hash stuff out, no one really saying how contrary-minded they might be feeling — trying for reason and consensus, and we go home feeling contrary, anyway.

Well, sometimes we form a committee.

✦

Cat pee and ketchup

THIS SMELL REMINDS ME OF SOMETHING, I say as Edwina and I lean into the salted herring that has marinated all fall out in the fish shed in vats the size of beds.

We're stuffing herring into net bags that will be spiked into the lobster traps. Sloosh, with a twist of the wrist Edwina stuffs the fish into the bag, rubber-gloves it shut, a fishtail poking out the opening, like her ponytail pokes out the back of her baseball cap.

I'm wearing my west coast union hat, with the jumping gold fish with the United Fishermen and Allied Workers Union logo, and a button from Melva, the button woman, that says United Fishers and Allied Workers Union, though the actual union hasn't changed to Fishers and that's the point of the button. Edwina's says Comeau Seafoods.

The dogs slide in to steal the bait bags, find secret places to roll in them, toss them in the air like dead rats, prance with them hanging in their mouths.

Edwina stiff-arms a bag of herring over her shoulder into the holding tank.

I worry the aroma like the dogs with the bait bags, nose left, nose right, eyes closed, quick sniffs. It's not just the smell, but the movement of our hands, scooping, dripping, pulling, our hair pulled back, the sucking sound as hands draw out a wet fistful.

Chickens, I pronounce, opening my eyes. Gutting chickens. Edwina makes a gross sucking sound, like the sound when you pull out the intestines.

Parker came over the other day, she says, reaching forward to rake in more fish. I'd decided it was time to kill a few roosters, especially the one that nearly beat me to death.

Well, Parker, he says wait, and he goes home and comes back wearing his old coveralls from the last time he went fishing. He's carrying a hammer handle for stunning them, and a little hatchet.

I look over at Edwina, up to her elbows in fish bait, and imagine her, pregnant and getting awkward, and Parker, 76 and wheezing, confronting these great whooshing roosters with wing spans of four feet.

Did you put the two nails on the block to stretch out their necks? I ask, while trying to imitate the finesse with which she stuffs the fish into the bag and secures the draw string.

Nope. Just whacked 'em. By the time we got done Parker was staggering around worse than the roosters. There was dust and blood and feathers everywhere. She backhands another bait bag over her shoulder, fish slime whizzing through the air with it. Parker, he doesn't like 'em to go quiet.

Parker doesn't want to go quiet either, I think. He

likes it when they jump and bounce around when it's over. No soundless draining in a bucket for him, pail weighted down with rock so it doesn't tip, necks down, wings bound by plastic walls. Not Parker, he wants them pumping, yelling, raising hell, bloodletting as they make their way out.

We've got about six roosters to go, she says.

I have been up to my elbows in guck the last two days, I say. Cleaned all the fat off that ham, and cleaned out that box of deer meat with the muscle all blasted with shot. We seem to live in slop.

Cat pee, she says, zinging a bag of fish over her shoulder.

Ketchup, I say, squeezing a herring like it's a plastic bottle.

Blueberry jelly, she says.

Diaphragm jelly and sperm, I say, waggling a fish.

Diapers, she adds. Don't forget diapers.

She stops to scratch her nose with a spot on her yellow rubber glove that isn't covered in fish scales.

Two nights ago I'm out at the village meeting, she says. Cecil's keeping house. Daniel says I have to pee, Dad, so Cecil says sure, you go ahead, the potty chair's right there, and keeps on watching his movie. He looks later and there's nothing in there, so he thinks nothing of it. I come home about 9:30 and start washing dishes, and I smell something funny, and here Edwina takes in a good noseful of air and says, I figure the septic must be backing up in the drains. We've got to dig a new septic, she says, grabbing another bag. There, 100.

Well, I can tell you when I got to the bottom of those dishes and found brown sludge, I was wild. Cecil, what the hell is this, I hollered and he comes in there to the kitchen wondering why I'm going on like a madwoman.

And then he gets to laughing, and he tells me what Daniel must have done. Well, I'm still half-wild, but I get to laughing, too, and there's the two of us standing in the kitchen with the smell of shit, then Daniel comes in. He doesn't know what we're gonna do. Then the three of us are standing there laughing like fools. The poor little guy was trying to help, emptying his potty like that. Emptied it right into the sink. I must have boiled those dishes four times on the stove before I figured they were clean again.

She grabs the edge of the vat, and steps down to the floor to swing up another bucket of empty bags. 850 to go, she says. Better speed up production.

We're standing up on platforms, slatted to let the water run through to the floor. We both wear gum-boots, and heavy knit sweaters and pants.

This is like the cannery I worked at in southern Alberta, I tell her while hauling in another netload of dripping dead herring. It was cold and wet, and we had to wear this same get-up.

Sounds like the fish plant, Edwina says.

Can you picture all these Ukrainian women, 30 or 40 years older than me, all of us in kerchiefs, sorting carrots and corn cobs? We were members of the Teamsters Union.

Edwina smiles.

The pay was good.

I'll bet.

They had these augurs that cut the niblets off the corn. No hand guards and sometimes someone's finger would go right in with the corn cob. Management would run down and race the woman off to hospital, then they'd figure out what batch of cans the finger ended up in, and take those off the line.

I'm never eating canned corn again, she says.

There now, I've done 100, I say, and grab more bags.

Picture us up there in this dark factory, standing on metal ramps, with one guy, sitting under a heat lamp drinking coffee and eating roast beef sandwiches. He runs the conveyor belt, and he's pushing us to work faster. Sometime in the middle of the night, I'd hear laughter spreading down the line, and he'd hear it too, and I'd lift my head to see a woman holding up a carrot for everyone to inspect.

Edwina already gets it and she's grinning.

Each woman would have stashed the most obscene carrot of the evening, stumpy things with knobs at the base, or long twisted ones, or double carrots. They'd start joking in Ukrainian over the roar of the machines, and as we passed the best carrots hand to hand, that man would speed up the belt. God we hated him.

You gotta do something for fun, Edwina says. Or
you go nuts in a job like that. At the fish plant, if a guy
whacked you with a dead fish, you'd stuff a handful of
fish eyeballs down his shirt. Then both of you'd go off
and think up the next rotten trick to play.

He'd glower at us, pour himself another coffee, he
always had hot coffee, and rev up the conveyor, while
we bent our heads to the task again, our aprons splat-
tered with corn cream and carrot juice.

Edwina biffs another bag behind her.

The manager was really bad at the fish plant. If it
was now, he'd get slapped with a sexual harassment suit
— but back in those days there wasn't that name for it.
I remember one woman chasing the guy with a hammer. You had to do something to give them the
message.

And so the day went on like that, the rhythm of
twisting wrists and twisting the truth, dipping into our
vats of fish and stories, waitressing and gutting bears,
lousy jobs and love affairs. We fill a thousand bags, her
700 to my 300, our clothes spattered with fish scales
and brine.

The next day, we pile into their red and white
Dodge half-ton, Edwina, Daniel, Amos and me — and
Smokey their cat who'd come back after three months
and everyone cried with happiness since they figured
he was dead, but now he has a big abcess. No room for
him up front so in he goes in the cat carrier in the back
with a blanket around the cage to keep out the wind.

The ferry crossing's rough and Edwina really guns that truck up the winding highway.

We drop Amos at Edwina's mum's, and I haul Smokey up front onto my lap before I realize the poor guy has peed all over himself in terror. We wipe him down, wipe me down, and fluff him up, drive into town with the windows down. Daniel's hungry so we stop at the Dairy Queen, take-out, and start out our day in town covered in root beer, pickles, ketchup and cat pee, with the ever-present overlay of fish.

Back in B.C., when we go to town, people say they know where we're from by the smell of woodsmoke on our clothes. Edwina tells me the best way to get the smell of fish off my hands is to scrub down with toothpaste. But I can see it could get into my skin.

✦

Bread and roses, chips and gravy

ONE DAY AT FRENCHY'S in Digby, Edwina has a full basket of clothes she's trying on, and I'm in the next dressing room, and we're tossing stuff back and forth over the partition — doesn't suit me, you try it — when we hear these older women talking out there by the bin of bathing suits and curtains, about being widowed.

I didn't know what to do with my time, said the first woman. I was so used to going with his time.

Catering to him, says her friend.

Yes, and for a while I didn't know what to do. Something would happen and I'd miss it and later I'd say, I could've gone to that! All those years I'd just go along with him and he'd decide.

You're not used to your freedom, says her friend.

All those years, he'd decide, says the widow.

Pause.

Now he's not here to do that.

Pause.

Nope, agrees her friend.

Cackle.

He wouldn't like this swimsuit.

Nope, says her friend.

Think I'll try it on, says the bereaved.

And then we're sorting through the shirt and sweater bins and you held up the purple shirt for me, and I said nope, I'm too chesty, and a woman we didn't know looked up and said to Edwina, wish I had her problem, and we all cackled.

Then we bought our stuff, Edwina with $45 worth and me with $1.50, hauled out, quick stop at the Irving for chips and gravy, travelling food, swivelling on the stools at the formica counter, teenagers, waitresses again on our day off.

✦

Breaking camp

LLOYD IS TAKING A PICTURE. To remember by. But
there is garbage in the bay. He props me in front of the
brier, the dog by my side, the wind at my back, ocean
and fish boats, but the sweetness is not roses.

Seven vultures lift higher, in the backdrop, wait for
us to finish so they can resume.

The flies hover over her — dead Jersey over the
rocks, down down below. Neck at the wrong angle, the
sweetness just beginning.

There is a place nearby named Cow Ledge, but no
cow has been there since aunts' and uncles' time. The
deer jump off there. Lloyd has seen them at low water
and slack tide, when the whole motion of the Bay of
Fundy stops, jump off the point of Cow Ledge to swim
across Grand Passage for Brier Island.

Near this ledge, back in the hill above, we come
across a hidden camp. It is one of many up and down
the shorelines, built by anyone who wants to get away,
no television, no phone, no demands.

Someone has burned this camp. The fire department thinks it's arson. Like a ruined home, with the
stench of blackened timbers, the camp is peeled open.
A tin stovepipe lies in pieces next to a charred couch.

The hardest pieces stick through the ashes — bed springs, broken pottery cups, and one elegant glass doorknob. Ruins of a home two young men built themselves, their camp where they went for parties, for sleep, for home. They built amidst the alder where once there was open ground and baseball games. The kind of camp we would find as children in another place and think they belonged to the old tramps off the railway. Now I am older and think of them as young. Breaking camp has a new meaning.

I wonder where the young people go who can't stand the smell of fish in their clothes, have to head west for the freedom, just as I've headed east for tradition. Or the kids who get chased away, like the one they went on about, calling him queer, and I laid into them like spreading hard cold peanut butter on soft bread, my anger in heavy smashing strokes, why are you trying to drive this kid out of town?

There are ruins of camps from years and years along this cove, high above the 27-foot tides. In one, we find asphalt shingles grown over, timbers scavenged from the ocean now fractured from rot and wind, a decomposed jacket, becoming a web in the ground, with one brass button remaining — the kind with a raised image of anchor and ropes.

This is where one group of boys camped, bonfires at night and bags of lobster — 50 pounds and they would feast and tell stories to fend off the wind.

This is where they dragged the raven chicks, daring

the high nests, scaring the parent, grabbing the baby, drag it behind the boat, and now, as parents themselves, know what they did, and never, ever, ever would do it again and it haunts them still.

Someone has led or hauled this cow to the edge, over the ledge. She wears a halter. Was she breathing when she went down? No, too uncertain a buffalo jump, an unreliable piskän. The vultures watch behind my right shoulder.

There is garbage in the bay and the dogs shouldn't go there. Bags of dead chickens, dumped for the gulls, sacks of pig fat, torn out and slopping, bed springs and bottles.

✦

That was a long time ago

HEY TONY, SAYS EARL CROCKER, you put up the money and I'll shoot for you, get you some Easter dinner. And Earl hoists up for Tony's benefit the two bags of ham he's just won in the Easter ham shoot in the field across from the farm with all the twirligigs.

Tony Thurber, Earl's brother-in-law and a crack shot, stands there in his orange jacket like a big blonde and trim Viking and roars. What'd Earl say? ask the other men who come in closer to hear the joke. Earl and Tony rock back and forth laughing, and you can see the rolling of the boat in their legs, and the kids are out in the field buying chances to shoot, and all the money goes to the volunteer fire department. Kids are eating chips, and the girls march around in clumps, a few taking their shots as well, and the new union representative chats his way around the circle.

The grass is the kind of long brown that comes in spring with the muck-holes of winter. There are no leaves budding yet. It's Easter, about one month since the former Baptist minister was charged with sexual assault.

Nine targets, photocopied bull's-eyes, are stapled up on the plywood board backed up against the begin-

ning of the spruce. Each contestant steps forward to
take a turn at their assigned target. Lifting the loaded
shotgun that is handed to them, they shoot, return the
gun, which is emptied, then reloaded. Everyone is
welcome to shoot. If you're new, like me, or a kid, they
might say, here, try the .410, it's smaller and lighter for
the first time. And if like me, you say, no, I've got two
layers of coat on, I can take the kick, they'll say fine, and
teach you how to hold the 12-gauge.

Earl's one of the men making the charges. There
are about 15 or 20 men, they were kids then, about the
age of the kids out here today in the field, and some
have moved away, and don't want to be known, and
some are here and don't want it known. Earl is encour-
aging them to say their piece.

Earl and Tony's laughter gathers others to them.
Earl's going to help out Tony, they repeat to the edges
of the circle, like a stone rippling on water. They're all
good shots, and the generosity in their teasing takes any
edge away from the quarrels of winter, as old and as
ready to be shed as the scruffy hair on a winter pony.

There is a certain rhythm to the loading, unloading,
stepping forward, the blast. The rhythm is not methodi-
cal, just a steady motion accompanying the sale of
chips, and people clomping their way to their trucks
over the bushes and the old fence, and the sound of
laughter on the wind as someone trips and lands in the
mud, and grips the hand held out to pull them up.

The court process is slow. After the 15 years of

waiting before anyone tells, or is believed, there is an almost overpowering amount of anger. There is prolonged emotion in this village where the daily rhythm of wind and tide, fish and ferries, baiting trawl and getting the kids ready for school is more likely to dictate the pace.

In the first moments of rage, the former minister's tires were slashed, and there was talk he'd been cut up for lobster bait. Then the process of preparing the case settled into meetings with the RCMP and more men coming forward. After the first preliminary court appearance, few attended any more — there was little to learn or report. One delay after the next, until the men would say, I have to go fishing, let me know what happened. Or, we'll hear on the news.

In his hospital bed, waiting for word from the court, Parker says that a long time ago there was suspicion something was going on, but the majority of the church advisory committee discounted the notion, and that was the end of it.

Earl and Tony are over comparing the pellet holes in their targets, and there's a small huddle around them. Earl got five holes and Tony got 34. We all look at my target sheet, no sign of any shot, and I try to sound nonchalant although secretly I'd hoped for a bull's-eye. Earl encourages me, Hey, you rattled the backboard. You could see the trees shake right back there. And I like his way of seeing things.

The process will get slower and slower, depending

upon the plea. If it goes to jury trial in this rural area, where the circuit court judge moves from district to district, the trial could be a year, even two, away, and they will all have to testify, go with their families up the island, across the ferry, up the Neck to the old red brick courthouse in Digby. Up the curved driveway on the side of the hill overlooking the scallop fleet in the harbour, up the cement steps to the main double doors, up the creaking wooden stairs to the courtroom, where the statue of blind justice is carved in wood behind the bench.

Down at his boat, Earl's face is a mixture of strain and pleasure as he screws down the ribbons, the strips of metal running the length of the boat that keep the hull from smashing on the wharf. A couple of friends drop by to comment on the extra strip he's adding, not usually seen on boats here. Earl smiles, spits out a bit of tobacco juice, offers a plug all round, and accepts the offers of help, as hands reach up and pull the ribbon down and around the curve of the boat. There's some good rocking kind of jazz on the truck radio. Earl's forecastle is freshly painted, grey and neat, not yet full of salvaged buoys, cases of oil, paper towels, life jackets and oilskins.

On the water, he says, you don't just see the water. You know the holes, the cliffs, and shoals, where the fish bank up certain times of year and tide.

Everyone went to the Young Peoples at the church — boys and girls. The minister took us bowling, swimming, we went on wiener roasts. But at pajama parties it was just the boys. I was sharing a bed with him when he tried something. I just rolled over and got out of bed. With others it was worse. But none of us talked to each other about it.

Later, at my kitchen table, Earl uses coffee cups to explain how the fishing fleet can find its way on the water. He explains how the Loran, the Long Range Navigation locater, works in the boat. He takes his coffee cup and mine, palms down over them, the back of one hand red and swollen. He lifts the cups, then sets them down precisely. The cups represent the towers that send out signals from the shoreline, the blue-and-white checked tablecloth the grid system on the ocean. The Loran picks out where the signals from the towers cross on the water, and locates your boat from there. Every area of the water, every buoy, has a locater number. In the fog when it's so thick you can't even see your hands, you have the Loran, the radar and compass, the sounder. The sounder will give you the depth, and because you know the ocean, you'll know where you are. If those systems fail, you'd still have the fog horn. There are always ways to get your bearings.

The minister would go from house to house. No one picked up the signals. Us kids used to just say keep away from him, he's a faggot. None of us said anything about what he did to us. We didn't understand then the difference between a homosexual and a molester. We just said he was a fruit, a queer, keep away. That was a long time ago.

I fish my own boat now. I've fished about 9 or 10 years full time, since I graduated. I'm 27 now. My boat is named the *Barb and George*, not my name. I've owned it for four years. It's 32-foot, fibreglass. Julie baits the trawl. We use Georgie's fish house, but we've just bought our own.

When we're longlining mostly we catch haddock. Sometimes you'll get a fish on every hook. Today on the second tide 95 per cent of them were dogfish, northern shark they're called sometimes, and he stretches his arms out a couple of feet, as wide as the table, to indicate their size.

They look like small shark, these dogfish. They have two horns that are poison. The fish will twist and thrash and the horns will poison you. There, you can see where the back of my hand is still swollen from where one horned me. Some people kill every one. They cut their heads off before they throw them back in. Or they slit their bellies to kill the pups they bear.

Later, mostly you never thought of it. Now and then, I guess. But you never really forgot it either. Then my fishing partner one day, on the lobster boat, tells me he heard it happened to someone, and I said it happened to me, and he said it happened to him, and then he said to hell with it, and went and reported it to the RCMP.

Some people do get poisoned. Sometimes badly. Sometimes it just lasts a few days. I don't let them get on the boat. I let them go alive, nip them off the hook at the rollers before they get aboard. But sometimes I kill them.

It happened to everyone, he says, so no one was left out in the cold.

✦

Brotherly things

1

MUM DIDN'T KNOW THIS, Andy says.

We had just moved to Brandon, and Donna, she must have been 10 or 11, she came home crying. There were red welts on her hand. Here she was, our little sister, and new to the school and didn't know the rules or anybody, and she must have said something wrong. They beat her, strapped her, humiliated her. Brutal bastards. They took her to the principal's office and strapped her.

I was 16, Andy says, and Brian was 18. Brian worked in the meat-packing plant, carrying carcasses on his shoulder, to earn money for university. He would come home shivering, cold for hours, his jackets soaked in sweat.

We went to the principal's office. Closed the door. Brian lifted the strap off the hook. It was a brown office. The strap was brown, too. Queen Elizabeth in the picture was blue, with faded yellows and greens. Brian slapped it across the desk where the principal sat, you brutal bastard when was the last time you got strapped if you ever touch our little sister again you will have us to answer to.

And mum never knew, because we didn't tell her. And the principal did not tell her either. And he did not touch our sister again.

I take up the tale, remembering another story. Mum learned kids at the school were getting strapped. She went into that school, 5'3", mother of five, the only sister of four brothers, one dead as a child, she walked into that principal's office, and she made a threat too. Not with the strap from the wall, but with her voice, her presence. You touch one of my children and you will have me to deal with.

There is a certain flatness of tone that means business, like the flat side of the field hockey stick, when there is no negotiating on this issue, when she knows the opponent has exhausted the store of manoeuvres, and she makes it clear she is only beginning to draw on the trouble she can cause.

2

Remember how you guys would write to the food companies, when you were 11 and 13?

Yes, on Brian's old typewriter, the old Underhill, and there were chipped letters and a faded ribbon. And we'd say we were young bachelors with disposable incomes, setting up on our own and having to decide which kind of brownie mixes we would be purchasing. If they wished for our future business, would they be so kind as to send samples. And they did, by the carton. Small bachelor-sized boxes, pale blue with darker blue lettering, and a brownie on the front.

Do you remember the time us girls broke into your boys only clubhouse in the back garage by the river flats and the old cars and you guys got so furious because we used the stolen money to buy ice cream cones? And didn't give you any? And so you went to mum? Only she said, if you boys are going to exclude the girls, you deserve it?

3

Do you remember the time you took me to the movies? Mum said you boys could go see the John Wayne movie, *Flying Tigers,* second on the double bill, if you'd take me to watch *Jack and the Beanstalk.* Don't you remember? When the giant chased Jack, I started screaming in the theatre, run Jack, run, run, and was crying and crawled under the seat and kept hollering from under there — Hey big brothers, take me home. I saw that John Wayne movie again just yesterday. All those Japanese pilots getting shot in the face.

4

And do you remember the time I found the pornography, in the house across the street, images so frightening, the woman cut in half with the table saw and being dragged away in two pieces across the stage that I still believe it was real? And you found it too, different books, magazines, but all the kids did probably in the neighbourhood.

From those days we learned our gender politics.

When the woman, Lorraine Mills, 24, in Sydney, in Nova Scotia, was stabbed to death by her boyfriend, months after she had spoken out about violence, you made sure we heard her voice long and hard on the TV news. You didn't show us bloody hallways, you showed us two reels of audiotape, turning round and round on the tape machine, and we looked into them as we would watch the wheels of the train, mesmerized, we were drawn in to her voice, this woman, whose blood was as real to me as the woman in the magazine.

5

It's funny about brothers, my mother said. You will be the little sister no matter how old you are, no matter how strong. My brothers are all over 80 and dying, she said, still angry at Glenn who died of emphysema, from smoking and he could have lived to age 95 like their mother, this brother she could have loved for 15 more years. And Ernie who is dying from Alzheimer's in Winnipeg, emaciated, strapped to a chair, who cannot remember anyone, this brother who sang barbershop in the tape of the family reunion, the brother who remembered all the music, all the words. And Hec who is dying in Saskatoon, the gracious and known man-about-town, coffee with friends at 10 every morning, golfing when he can.

She said, I know I was always their little sister, but I wonder, as they grew older, did they make the time to be together, say I love you when they could?

Love you, brother, I heard Cecil say to Lloyd one night in Nova Scotia. Love you, too, was the return.

✦

Bent pins and broken needles

A FRIEND BACK HOME showed me a small tobacco tin, the oblong upright kind. In the spidery script of an old woman's hand, with yellowed tape holding it down, the label read: Bent pins and broken needles. My friend shook the tin, then pried off the lid, and as we looked into it together, she said: When she died I couldn't bear to throw them away.

Shirley McMullen lowers herself into the rocking chair behind the music stand, where a crochet magazine opens to her latest orchestration. She holds the crochet hook as if it is her bow, the strings the lines of intricate notes, her life the symphony she conducts.

She points her hook at her crocheted creations, then spreads her hands to encompass their breadth. Like Shirley herself, they are substantial, well-thought-out pieces of work. They cover claw-footed tables, entire beds. Across the back of the couch, long-bladed skaters, hands held behind them, cut and stride. Here in this house, with Shirley, her books and maps and porcelain cats, I can almost hear the blade cut the ice, the wind on hair and cheek, as my mother flies along the frozen Assiniboine, or the Red.

Her bookshelves run from ceiling to floor. She shows me books she couldn't bear to leave behind, the one her great aunt gave her, published in 1885, and the Shakespeare her grandfather gave her when she was eight years old. In the copy of *Little Women* she selects for me, there is no publication date. My hands, as if reading braille, explore the surface, as if it is a continent, the red fibres of the hardcover the roughness of the prairies, rippled with words like rivers of silver and gold. We stand together between the bookshelves and the rocking chairs, exploring the pages of Canadian History Notes from 1899, with the maps of Assiniboia, Ungava, the District of Franklin, Keewatin, the land I have crossed not knowing the old names, these waters my father explored as a young botanist.

Her station by the picture window gives perfect access to the village, and the village perfect access to her. She considered buying my brother's house, but declined the isolation. Seventeen porcelain cats, chickens, ducks and an elephant share the view. Balls of yarn: red, purple, and coral, flow from wicker baskets. Mauve flowers on slender stems blossom amidst shamrock leaves. Her trophies — cribbage, 20; darts, 5; and pool, 10; speak of foursomes of friends huddled nights around Legion tables in the Freeport winter, or the sharp eye and sure hand guiding the cue.

The stilted words, like a long-gone language, an archaic style, like mental cultivation and physical recreation, like bent pins and broken needles, are the phrases given to me here.

Shirley's life, transplanted, took hold with old books and new stories. She spends little time on the husband who left her for a younger woman. Instead, she talks of the men and women who listened to her, the new-comer, the woman whose kids had grown up and husband gone, with a house so ripped apart in this new life that you could see through the walls. How she went down the road to board with Gloria Howard, like kin, who works at the Legion, too, and has raised her own kids alone.

Shirley's four grown-up boys thought she'd suffer the emotions of the loss but not the loss of the money.

But it was the other way around. And as she talks of it, she speaks of her mother, in Quebec, who was divorced early, raised Shirley, and in those years — Shirley realizes as she crochets and talks — she learned she could manage, too. Those years her mother worried for her, maybe getting pregnant, and Shirley saying, Don't worry, mother, no man's touching me until I'm married. And she leans forward, tells me the time she was 19 and the guy training her at the CPR, in the accounting department, he pulls up close to her as if to give her instructions, and slides his hand onto her knee, and Shirley, she raises an arthritic hand to show me how high she slammed from, and whack, she hits the arm of the rocker as if it were his hand there now, and you hear his shock reverberate through the hall as her 250 co-workers begin to clap.

Shirley settles back into the rocker, unwinds more yarn.

As her kids grew, before she came here, she was a Cub leader. She taught survival skills — fire-fighting, camping and gardening, first aid, and service to community. Now she's 61, organizes tournaments for the Legion, and owns her own home which is like a drop-in centre. Sometimes ten coffee cups are stacked at her kitchen sink from the people who drop by to visit or to work on the always-present jigsaw puzzle — lupins, fishing boats, maples.

She talks of missing the wail of the trains of Quebec, but how the foghorn helps. She talks of her work at the fish plant, and of the boarders she took in — single men, and women who had left their boyfriends or husbands. She tells stories of differing personalities and shared meals.

She tells of the rumours spread because she gave a home to unmarried or separated women. That she was running a whorehouse. That this was a home for battered women — unlicensed. That she was a bootlegger — she could hardly wait to tell her mother that one.

The outside door into the kitchen opens and her friend Gloria comes in.

She's picking my brains, Shirley tells her. Only I told her she can't use some of the stuff I said. Like what, asks Gloria. About the whorehouse and the bootlegger, Shirley says, and Gloria sinks into a chair next to Shirley and they sit laughing together.

✦

Family ties

I THINK ABOUT SHIRLEY'S arthritic and skilled fingers during the weeks I fret over my quilt square. The quilting bee is my first invitation to a women's event, and I want to meet more women.

The hearts I sew and stuff are puckered and taut. I have never done applique, and Edwina has tried to advise me. This reminds me of grade seven, where I ripped and resewed a placket zipper until the sea green cloth of the A-line skirt was a grubby embarrassment. These purple hearts on yellow cloth, with my name stitched crookedly and in anger at my own ineptitude, seem a shabby tribute to a child. Edwina has tried to encourage me, but I am not a complete fool, and she has the grace to laugh when we stand looking at this mess.

At the quilting bee, eleven women and three children gather in the room looking out over the cove. The tide is coming in. We have been invited, by the woman who is an ambulance attendant and midwife, an artist of quilts and earrings and sculpture, to come here to sew the baby quilt together. Edwina cannot attend, but sends her square, swiftly stitched panels depicting the schoolhouse, where the mother-to-be is a teacher.

This small wooden house is heated with a wood stove. The doorframes facing the ocean are painted deep pink. A woman's house, I thought, the first time I drove by. The rest of the siding is weathered and grey. Inside, there are quilts on frames, and sculptures of wood and glass and wool. Children dig into a suitcase full of toys. The suitcase is painted with stars and the night sky, it reminds me of conjurers, and circus tents, the smell of sawdust and things I'd like to understand.

We take our turns at the quilt, some women skilled, some clumsy-fingered. As the work goes on, and women take their place, then pass the needle to the next, I find myself by a woman I have never met.

She is a teacher, her hair blonde and neat, her pantsuit robin's-egg blue. She is trim and holds a cane loosely. She asks where I live and what I do. She tells me she once lived in my brother's house. Nettie Cameron is her name. She speaks to me in words controlled like a painter gripping her brush too tightly.

The baby quilt is purples and yellows, aquas and reds. Make hearts if you like, we were told, and those of us without nimble fingers tugged and knotted our purple cloth, puckered and sweated, not knowing how our grandmothers and sisters could find this relaxing. Those with skill and fleet fingers stitched lace hearts and tiny perfect blocks of words — FAMILY TIES, they said.

I ask Nettie which one she's done, and she points to five bright balloons — purple, yellow, and criss-cross patterns, that float on the square. The woman she boards with has tied down the strings for the balloons. The strings seem to anchor what might otherwise float away.

We stood on the side, watching and admiring as the experienced quilters completed the difficult parts. Out on the cove on the Bay of Fundy the tide was close to full. It seems now, long after, that there was so much fullness that night, such swelling, that there was some need to empty.

When I moved here, she says, I had nothing. This was five years ago. I'd split up with my husband, come here alone and didn't know anyone. That's when I rented your brother's house for not much money but had to leave after a few months. Just packed everything in the car. At the next island, they said come stay here and we'll find a job for you at the library. So I did. I ended up living with a man. I don't know how. One day he just moved my stuff in with him. And I stayed there until I left.

You worked for radio, she looks at me and I nod. I did some work for radio, too, she says. For Annapolis Valley Radio, AVR. In their newsroom. And I did some pieces for CBC. They didn't pay much, but I would have done it for free. It's like an addiction. It's all I wanted to do. They paid me $65 for the piece on whale watching, enough to take both my daughters out on the boat with me, to make a day of it. Once they put me in a little room to cut tape on big editing machines. I didn't know how to do it. I cut the tape so close with the razor blade that you couldn't catch the first part of things.

I couldn't stop doing interviews. Once I did a 10-minute piece for AVR for Remembrance Day. I interviewed 90 veterans in their homes. I didn't get paid much. A First World War veteran talked about mustard gas, how they didn't know what it was in the beginning. I talked to a woman veteran. I talked to flyers. They invited me into their homes and we sat at their kitchen tables. I worked on it for weeks. I didn't want to do anything else.

You understand this obsession, she says. Again, I nod.

By now, the quilters have completed their work and moved into another room. The quilt frame is removed. We sit on two chairs in the emptied space.

My 16-year-old daughter committed suicide. Judy, her name was. Is. That's three years ago now. I try not to think of it all the time. She was going with a fisherman. He was older. He drank. She wasn't used to that. I don't know if she did it to get back at him or what. But it threw me for a long time. I've learned something. I didn't get the kids because I didn't have money. I didn't want to take them from their home or from their father, who they adored. Now I know I could have done as good a job. I try to keep busy. It's good that I am teaching now. I would like to think of myself as a writer. But I'm not. I don't do it full-time. So I can't call myself a writer. You could listen to my tapes if you want.

The first summer in Freeport was so hard, she says. At first my girls were here. Fiona was only 13. She worked at the fish plant so she could be with me. I remember her walking home from work with her little apron dragging on the ground. By the next year, everyone had picked up. We weren't all living together, but we'd settled. Things seemed fine. Judy died that fall.

I wanted to touch her. I did touch her. I wanted to make sure she was okay, even if she was dead. On her tombstone it says Judith, but she was Judy.

I mumble on. I have to talk. I know some people call me Nuttie Nettie, but they let me talk. They're good to me.

But it is strange for me tonight that we are here for a woman having a baby and I have lost my baby. I love the kids on this island. They talk to me and tell me things about themselves. Real things. They're the most loving children. I substitute in any grade, in any subject, so I know them all. They are sensitive. I can say to the kids, no I can't do that, it reminds me too much of Judy. I extend my family to the kids. There is so much physical contact here. That's why the minister was such a shock. Everyone trusted him.

I love the kids. One day a student came and put her arm around my neck, practically lifted me over to the window in a hammer lock. Look, she said, if one person sees a crow, it's bad luck. If two see it, it's good luck. Thanks, Mrs. Cameron.

✦

Sloughing off

IN THE DREAM, Caroline said you've finally found the time to be with friends.

In the dream that is set in my home in the mountains, she said, I stopped coming here because friends weren't important. Meetings were. Phone calls. They were the items you could check off your list. Time with friends to you was sloughing off.

The day of the dream I am sitting against the outside wall with Edwina, 3,000 miles from Caroline, in the nook away from the wind as Amos in diapers launches himself into the swimming pool, full body-check into Daniel, and the dog races circles under the flapping laundry.

Edwina tells me she is pregnant, that she is glad I have been here as her neighbour. The phone rings inside, but she does not answer. We are hidden in a nook, in the sun, from passing cars and phone calls. We both know I will leave soon. I may have cried a little, or maybe it was the wind.

These dreams, these women, I understand now, help me to slough off. To shed, like a snake, a vileness, an itching grasping illness. To slough off nightmares that pull me back, and lists to keep me steady, chores and TV to keep me skimming, like roast beef that calms, deeds with rewards, the daily measure, the daily dose, the phone ringing and demands met.

I thought about how one woman, Shirley, has found her place, with a home and endless friends. There are few sharp edges anymore, except the ones that can be laughed at together. And I expect that Nettie will get to tell her story to strangers and friends again and again until it doesn't hurt so much anymore, a lost finger, a lost child, like Edwina said, the pain won't ever go. But the time will come when the scars, like the friends, are the signs of survival. And you learn to trust that your survival gear will keep you afloat.

✦

Ebb tide, Flour Cove, 7:45 am, Sunday, near Freeport, Bay of Fundy

THESE ARE THE COLOURS.

Basalt in large pillars, ledges grey and red in the morning sun.

Rockweed the colour of ochre.

Tall grass, purple vetch, wild blackberry to the edge of the rock. Seed-heads on the grass.

Wildflowers on the rocks, large and pink and shaped like petunia, strangely domestic, the colour of a candy-striper's uniform.

Spruce thick, dead and black to the top of the rocks, bent away from the wind and water. The spruce is stripped, as if there has been a fire, and the force of the wind is in them, even when the air is still.

Dying clover, past their season.

Gulls and crows.

A flash of light off the glass of one boat.

A man walks down to the shore. I've seen him on the road. This is his ocean to check each day, not mine. My dog barks, stands by me. The man waves.

Wild peas with flowers the colour of fuchsia, spread over the rocks, wild pinks and purple with their sweet peas by now bitter in brown pods.

Evidence of campfires, charred heaps on the rock

where white and yellow and red lichen meet the pink seams of granite. Old fires are strewn with nails and spikes from the driftwood.

A tuft of black dog hair in the rocks. Bits of newspaper from firelighting. Two Pepsi cans. One styrofoam cup.

In a tidal pool, a plastic bottle stands upright, swaying slightly in the wind, as if it's had enough to drink.

Another truck, grey like mine, drives down to the water, and another old man comes down to check the ocean. The dog runs out to bark. The wind is cold, and Connor runs back to me, lies behind my hip, keeps me warm, my big black solar collector.

High on the barren places, wild roses mass against the wind, and down in the crevices small bluebells on slender stems find shelter.

In the receding water, huge rocks stand dripping with rockweed, like woolly mammoths emerging from the sea.

Only the yellow lichen grows in circles, like potato prints or an old language.

◆

Edges

IT SEEMS, SOMETIMES, that I am trudging to the edges. To the prairie wind, that cuts the brain, to the Atlantic, that won't say summer, to the snow that threatens to kill.

In a movie I saw, the old woman, her death coming soon, in her singsong Scandinavian recalls the flood and ebb of her river. She says the hardest parts of life are the most exciting. She is dying and she is smiling, because she is facing the hard part.

The nature of power is in the unleashing, it seems to me, the stripping away of compromise. It is the woman giving birth where she chooses, the giving or taking of life, the suicide, the end of the binding. I have not borne children, and do not know that kind of power — wrenching of flesh and flesh. Such power of life and death I have only known in other ways, where the peace of transformation comes too, I believe, in the giving over, the giving to, the transfer of spirit, the deliverance.

That power at the edge I have met in the morgue, where the burial society prepares bodies for burial or cremation. That power comes also at the butchering of the bear, its power large, the kind that makes dreams for years. It is there at the killing of a chicken, the ridiculous squawking that isn't, not really. The gutting of a fish, steeling ourselves to their hundreds.

There is power at the edge, when the body gives way to bloodiness and pain each month. When the cells swell, when the anger swells, when there is no longer room for lies or pretence, when the body's only desire is to push, push away, persons, if they come too close, objects, if they get in the way, will push past them, unleashed, like the wind and storm waters, will not stop for discussion or reason, will flood, smash, and destroy, until it finds the edge where truth cannot be papered over, until it can subside, eventually, quiet a while, make peace.

At the edges the truths lie, but we cannot live on that sharpness forever.

Later, we can leash ourselves again, create structure, new runners to support the arches, new hairdo to tame the edges, buy a new bra, a good one from the Bay. Then there is a desire to smile, prepare supper, work things out.

✦

Pulling together

JAMES KEELAGHAN TELLS US on the radio today while I'm cleaning the truck that we should go to a place we've always wanted to go. Do it while you can, he said.

Teams from Valley and Southwest Nova represented, says the Canada Day ad in the *Clare Shopper*. Oxen pull at the Weymouth fairgrounds. And then further down the French Shore the 225th anniversary of the Acadian settlement of Clare. Two events on the same day, a part of Canada I have never met.

I ask friends to go with me, but am happy to be travelling alone again, talking to strangers.

In the evening I return home sunburnt and happy. I have eaten french fries (they don't call them chips here) and Rappie pie and Canada Day cake. I have driven out of fog and into sun, crossed ferries, driven by fields of lupins, understood Acadian French, been told stories and told stories, talked politics, been welcomed even when my French faltered, learned how oxen pull heavy weights, and did not hear a single American accent. I have never been happier on Canada Day.

In the town of Weymouth, there are yard sales everywhere. At the dusty fair grounds, families have set up rummage tables. A tinny loudspeaker blares out "Fare-well to Nova Scotia", and other Canadian songs, while at the Kinsmen Hall local recreation groups sell raffle tickets for a quilt.

We're watching the oxen pull.

From my spot on the bleachers I see men and women wearing hats that say Case International, UltraMar, Gilbert's Cove, N.S., 7-Up, Mail-Star, Lewis Sawmills. The Lewis Sawmills float arrives back from the parade route, and I smile at sight of the three huge round sawblades mounted on top. Behind it comes the entry from the local steam cleaners, an old claw-foot bathtub mounted on a truckbed. An old man drives a bright green 1957 International truck, obviously his pride, and young girls with batons run into the fair-grounds. There are black people speaking French, there are white people speaking French, there are black and white people speaking English and French.

The couple beside me now — they're retired air force. He's from Quebec and she's from here in Weymouth. Can you see the lights of Yarmouth from Freeport, he asks? No, I can see the French Shore I say, but the curve of the province hides the lights of Yarmouth. When we lived in Moose Jaw, he says, we could see the lights of Regina, 40 miles away in the night sky.

They have lived across the country — in B.C., Saskatchewan, Nova Scotia, Quebec, Alberta. They've been to the oxen pull before.

I've never seen this, I say.

You're not from here, he says.

No, from B.C.

Oh, I know what you have there. Salmon pull, he says with his strong French accent and it sounds like sollmun. Salmon, he says again and we laugh as the little girls next to us, who've come from Yarmouth to be in the parade, show us some of their baton routines up there on the bleachers and I try one out, the moves coming back in the memory of the muscles.

We already favour one young man and his oxen. He is maybe 14. It is obvious his oxen, deep rich brown with red and gold ornaments on their foreheads, like the foreign and rich colours of a middle-Eastern dancer, love him. Two other men compete, one a solid man whose team works hard. And a third man, who hollers at the team, shoves, hits their faces. They are clearly the strongest animals in this round of the small oxen. Their shoulders arch, and they pull round after round as more weight is added.

The old man who drove the 1957 International in the parade lumbers up with his plate of barbecued chicken. I bet you can't eat all that, I say to him as he hefts himself up into the third and top row next to me.

A lot of years I couldn't afford to buy half a chicken, he says. His hat says Sissiboo Electric, Weymouth, Nova Scotia. You bring 12 kids to the fair, you give them all the money for rides.

I raised 12 children, and three more after that. And now I got 42 grandchildren. My wife keeps baking for that many and I keep eating it, he says, pointing to his stomach. When you're old you can't burn it off.

Each block weighs 200 pounds, he says. Together, we count 15 blocks. After each team pulls, a yellow front-end loader from Lewis Sawmills, with a red balloon tied to it, hauls the blocks back into position.

The drag against the ground counts for another thousand pounds. He tells us nobody here is doing this for the money. It costs a lot to raise these animals. And they will maintain more than one team.

You're from Freeport, are you? he says. I worked there. I worked in the fish meal plant — under Parker Thurber.

I know Parker, I say.

You tell him hello. He'll remember me, he says, and tells me his name.

The tops of my feet are burning, and the woman asks her husband to go get the lotion from the car. When he returns, she tells me to turn sideways, and she massages the lotion onto my neck.

In B.C., they were so friendly when we got there, her husband says. In summer, they would open the door for you and smile, and I thought, oh good, this is just like Nova Scotia. But in winter they slam the door. It got so dark and closed, they closed up, too. They were like different people.

It's a hard place to live sometimes, I say. For me, I was so involved in politics, I couldn't write.

You girls must be happy Kim Campbell got in, he says.

The woman says she would have backed Charest, because Kim Campbell won't get the support of the men she needs to win.

No, he says, we got a good system in this country, but some people take advantage.

I've been around long enough to recognize a small piece of bait when I see one, and smile at his offering. Like corporations, I say, rising slightly and smiling down at the oxen.

You take them away and what do you have?

Seems to me a lot of them take our money and leave with it, I counter, cheering for the boy.

Neither of us want to go further with this on this day.

He offers a compromise and we both smile. Our team is pulling well, and we focus back on them.

The young man and his oxen are trying to pull 4600 pounds. They lurch forward with the weight and I clap, out of turn. Everyone else knows this doesn't qualify. He hasn't pulled the distance. He makes the second allowed attempt, rounds his oxen back into place. Leans into their faces, whispers something, and they pull for him and everyone claps. The oxen have said this last one's for you, and he knows it and we all know it, and he is sweet-faced and kind.

We all leave the bleachers. We've seen the young animals pull and the sun now is too strong.

I decide to drive down the French Shore to Meteghan, the place where the boatyard repairs the dragger. They're celebrating Canada Day in their high school, as part of their 225th anniversary. There will be traditional Acadian music. This celebration is for themselves, not a tourist attraction, though all are welcome.

The large gymnasium is full. My French is poor, but I can pick up some phrases in context. When a chair empties after I've stood near the entrance a long while, a woman gestures for me to sit near her. As chairs open closer to the middle, she ensures that I move with her. She points out the events in her program so I can follow. I am clearly not from this neighbourbood, but she still doesn't know I am English. A woman is called up front to place the star on the map of Clare where her family settled 225 years ago after the expulsion of the Acadians from Grand Pré. She wears a white cap tied beneath her chin, a cotton skirt and bib apron. The woman next to me exclaims, awaits my response, but I don't understand what she says, or what has been said of the woman in the dress.

I'm sorry, I say. I have very little French.

She wears her grandmother's wedding dress, she says, smiling a welcome to me. When she and her husband shift closer again to the centre, she pats the seat next to her again. I almost cry at her kindness. I think later that people who have been displaced themselves are the kindest hosts.

We watch a family of eleven play a reel, we watch their best step dancers. We eat *gateau-anniversaire*, of Clare and of Canada. We eat Rappie pie in the sun.

✦

Measurements

THESE ARE MY MEASUREMENTS, I say.

38-32-41

These are mine, he says. And he draws me to the window, between the filing cabinet and the bathroom door. I know in the spring the sun rises behind the garage, there, on the right, over the fields where you saw them burning the grass.

Then taking my hand, he leads me to the living room. Where it sets is there, just there up on the ridge, way to the left of your brother's house, up where you found your Christmas tree.

On the longest days of summer, when we're fishing, I go out back early, take my cup of coffee, sit on the cover of the septic tank, and the sun comes up over the spire of the church. It sets out over the Bay of Fundy, and we'll walk there, or go down in the truck, and sometimes see the whales spouting.

There is a marker, an old post, up there near your house, at the edge of the field where the property line is. That's where we run our ropes. When we're repairing traps, running the new lines, it's exactly 100 fathoms from the fish shed, right across the road and over the field to that wooden post. I've done it for years. Every fall when we get the traps ready for lobstering.

And when you are gone, I will pace that field every day, measuring my loss.

✦

Softball

EDWINA COULD NEVER GET AWAY for softball, kids to mind, village meetings, new well getting drilled. And there we were like Field of Dreams with the fog rolling in, and the women and the softball disappearing in the mist, you could just hear the drunk at the side in the fog hollering at us that we were cows, I told him to go f___ himself, only I didn't say "f". And the other drunk from the visiting team's fan club, who told my buddy when I was standing there that he, my buddy, should tell me to get my ass out there and play ball. And I said to my buddy, who seemed to be the intermediary, and besides I liked the parallel structure, that he should tell his friend to go f___ himself, and I didn't say "f" then either. I mean, harassment is harassment, and even if I was the oldest on the team and had hardly, unless you count that one game for the NDP, ever played before, I wasn't taking that shit.

So I got out there and wiggled my butt like they do on TV baseball at the Legion, raised the bat and whacked it. Grounder to left field. Not like Elli Jo who could swing so casually and knock them into the far grass and hummocks. But respectable. Except for the time I got tagged on the way to first, and they played a double and my dog bounded out on the field howling to protect me, and I was laughing and crying, and Donna and Annette, who I barely knew, put their arms on my shoulders when I couldn't stop crying and said hey, it's only a game, we all get out, only I couldn't say, it's not that, it's not that. It's that I'm leaving next week, leaving this field, leaving my brother, my lover, my friends, this sky, because I have to go home again. I want to. I need to.

So I haul in a breath, stride to outfield, and catch the first goddamn ball I have ever caught in my life, and roll in the grass like a filly kicking her legs up, and both teams are laughing and hollering, and no one even cares that I won't let go of the ball, hold it like a goalie, and the other team got onto second while I jumped around the shortstop with the ball in my hand.

Last night on the phone, Edwina in Nova Scotia and me back in B.C., we decided if we ever get an elected Senate with gender parity, then we'll each run, and end up in Ottawa together with fat paycheques and a pension, and start a Senate daycare and softball team.

◆

Splicing

HOW DO WE SPLICE OUR LIVES, frayed ends wanting to curl around each other from two sides of this country. How do we bring together these thousands of miles, say we aren't so far apart, we can do it, we have friends and homes and children, we have fish and gardens, grain, timber and songs. What we want to say is yes, and we don't know if it will work. We just want to say yes and keep trying. We want to splice together our winding highways, through the fog, along the water, let our frayed pieces, pulled and stretched, touch at the prairies, cauterize with a wildfire, cool in a prairie wind blowing from British Columbia to the Maritimes, a giant piece of rope, stretching from the docks of our oceans, and in the middle, we will find the strength to pull harder, begin to turn, with our short and calloused fingers, splice one piece through the other, until we are together, stronger than two hands entwined.

✦

Familiar highways

WE BOTH MAKE OUR TREKS to Nana.

On the phone last night mum says on her 74th birthday, that they went to Scotland, where they walked the Royal Mile, between Holyrood Castle and Edinburgh Castle, the route Nana, as a ten-year-old, ran each day. The child worker, a seamstress' assistant, running the dresses for royalty between the castles. Running the Royal Mile in 1902.

I only wish I could tell her I walked in her footsteps, Mum says.

There is a straight line of women. I can see the profiles, at a dance at our community hall, the mother, daughter, granddaughter, talking, laughing, watching; the profiles of their cheekbones, or the line of pictures on my wall — mum a child by the picket fence in La Riviere, you can see the rip in the old photo, this only picture of herself as a child, standing in the mud in 1924 with the kewpie doll she hated but had to hold for the black and white picture. She wears black leggings, hair cut straight across in bangs. And Nana, at 90, hands together in her lap, white hair, her dress flowers of browns, creams and oranges, the afghan behind her the zigzag patterns of oranges, blacks, greys and creams.

There is a straight line of women. We sit together at the theatre, stealing illegal licorice from a capacious handbag. The Reese's peanut butter cups we unwrap stealthily, an eye on the patrolling usher at the theatre where we flout the rules, bring in our own candy. We spend $7 on popcorn and pop, our cover, my sisters and mother, laughing all the way to and from the junk food section of the grocery store across the intersection. In age we range from 38 to 73, a straight line of women, going to the early show, 5:30, it's cheaper and we're not used to staying up so late. After all, we are going for supper after the show. Whoopie Goldberg, *Sister Act,* and the small theatre at 5:30 is almost all women, giggling and passing candy.

Later on my trip, in Edmonton, we pick up our friend and her sister. Four of us, women, one of us dying of breast cancer, we go to see *League of Their Own,* laughing and hollering for the women, our team.

At the Baptist Church children's Christmas program, in Freeport, I sit alone in a pew behind a row of old women. Their hair is white and gentle. Two wear poinsettia earrings, the other wears red plastic bells hanging from holly leaves. They watch the children, laughing and whispering, my row of Nanas.

I do not know many stories of Nana. I know she always made extra muffins because the neighbourhood kids were always hungry. I know she kept a secret from the days she worked in the castle. She saw something through a heating grate between the floors. Something she would never tell not even 80 years later. I know in Winnipeg that Stanley Knowles used to come to meetings at her house, where the men talked CCF politics, and Gramp was in the meetings, and Nana served the men sandwiches and left the room. I know that when Gramp figured they should live in the country and there they were in La Riviere, with Nana up on some hill with no water and in an old log house with five kids, and dressing them in old flour sacks, and Gramp thinking the rural life was the way to live except he was always off on the railway, that's when I know Nana packed the chickens in crates, and the kids in the Model A, and drove that familiar road into Winnipeg. Gramp could keep the farm if he wanted; she wasn't doing the romantic bit of rural life while he was gone all the time. You come here if you want me was the message.

And Nana must have thought of her own mother, my great grandmother. After 10 grown kids, she packed up and left her husband on the Isle of Man. She took the youngest child with her, and left for New Zealand, where, still being a Catholic, she could not divorce or remarry, so became a bigamist.

And then sometime along the way there, when my own mother had five kids, and almost all grown, and she couldn't stand it in Brandon any more, not one more year after the next, not her place any more, couldn't stay there any more for the kids or the job or the safeness, she packed up, too, you come with me this time if you want me.

And there's something in this long line of women, saying you come to me this time if you want me. Because I'll make my home where I go, and will not always follow you. Sometimes you'll have to follow my heart. I am beginning to see the thread in this long line of women.

✦

A well-seasoned traveller

IN WINTER, DO NOT EAT a meal consisting of boiled cauliflower, boiled potatoes and steamed white fish. I learned this in 4-H. In winter, we do not need to look over our white plate of white food past a white tablecloth through a frozen windowpane at a snowbank. Add a sprig of fresh parsley, if available, or a sprinkle of paprika.

Dec. 4, 1991 *The Digby Courier*
Out and About
[Excerpts]
BEAR RIVER NEWS — by Beryl Henderson —
Mrs. Evelyn Steadman flew to Ottawa to visit her son and wife, Brian and Lillian Davey. Later on they motored to Guelph, Ont., and had dinner with Evelyn's nephew, then on to Rockwood, Ont. Evelyn visited four cousins, two of whom she had not seen since 1924.

Then they went to Britannia, Ont., where Evelyn had lived from 1919-1927. There she met long time friends Mr. and Mrs. Madill. Mr. Madill is a clockmaker and has a large collection of clocks. He wears one on his cap and has a large clock on his barn.

Evelyn also visited the Mohawk racetrack. She goes there once a year and won 8 out of 9 races by choosing horses with odd names.

Then she returned to Rockwood and left on the Gold Bus October 11th to go to Ajax. Her youngest grandson, Carl Davey, met her and they motored back to Ottawa on Friday.

A family gathering was held for Thanksgiving with turkey and all the fixings. On Tuesday, (her son) Bruce took Evelyn to his favourite restaurant for a roast beef dinner. The next morning, Bruce took her to the airport at 6:30 a.m. and she returned to Halifax. She came back to Riverside Manor in Bear River the next evening, a well-seasoned traveller.

I would like some days to be Mrs. Evelyn Steadman of Bear River, to appear in the "Out and About" column of the *Digby Courier*, a visitor noted and welcomed. I once laughed at such things. Like the wedding announcements, the 4-H column, who is visiting who. Now it matters to me. That we know that her son and daughter-in-law picked her up and took her to dinner with her nephew and, at the end of the trip, after she'd bet on horses at the Mohawk racetrack, she returned to her old hometown and met her friend the clockmaker. That they gathered all the family together in their home and made her a turkey supper, and the next night her son took her to his favourite restaurant for a roast beef dinner. It matters to me that he took this woman I don't even know to the airport early the next morning (I can imagine the excitement of the early night before, Evelyn Steadman returning home on the 6:30 flight), and she flew half-way back across the country and she met her old friend and they visited that friend's husband in the hospital, stayed overnight with her daughter-in-law's mother and then came back to the Bear River Manor the next morning, to her own home town, where her journey would be honoured and relived and read about by people she doesn't even know.

✦

Living room, Bay of Fundy, 4:15 pm

PUT ON THE CONNIE KALDOR prairie tape.

Start the warm-ups; the arms, triceps, biceps, get the heart moving, because *the heart is bigger than trouble* and you gotta keep moving, the exercise keeps you from getting down, especially in February. Make yourself move, get warm, out of the snow, the wind, the unemployment, friends dropping, exploding, imploding, keep moving, move it. Into the fast stuff, you're riding over the prairie, fast fast, jump on that pony, race the train, skip town, be an outlaw, outrun hate behind you, and in you. *I can ride, I can shoot,* says the outlaw, and by now I am panting, running, no one can outsmart me, I'll only be gotten if I want to be, knowing I am wanted is better than being had, and my heart is thundering and the music moves into a swinging waltz, into Carberry on my way across Canada, and I smile at *the clock flippin' ads on the wall* in Al's cafe, and I'm lifting weights to the clock's time, and the feeling of *home, home, home.* I take the pressed-back chair, choose to look out the back window with its tall prairie grass and clothesline and beyond it the Bay of Fundy, while Connie Kaldor sings of farms and the parents left behind. Lift the leg, move it. Nana, you left the farm.

You left your husband. Move it. Mama, you left the prairie town, you left your husband. Move it. Great nana, you left the country, you left your husband. Moved it. And then we relax into the waltz, and the swing, the *bird on a wing*, and I'm a waitress again, frying eggs at the Greyhound, pushing out lunches at the El Rancho, ladling soup for the poor people who bought a bowl of soup at the Golden Gate and filled it with ketchup and crackers. You gotta keep going, digging into the coins in the white nylon pockets, you gotta do it, move it, even if it's February and the roads are snowed in, and it's five in the morning, and there's mudslides down the mountain, and there's no help to jump the car, and the pipes are frozen, you gotta keep going. Push it.

◆

The well-seasoned traveller
needs roast beef sometimes

SOMETIMES SHE EVEN NEEDS to stop awhile and save potato water. She grows weary of constant change, precarious dining, adventure. While she may rapidly tire of marital arguments to which she is privy in the homes of her friends, as a guest of the household, she is grateful for a moment's rest from the road, where baseball spirits invade one's domain. She longs to watch kittens at play, to let the dog from its leash, to watch the snow fall without fear of collision.

The well-seasoned traveller appreciates a good audience, one which is not travel weary itself, cannot outdo her stories of catastrophe or nonchalance, whose children grow wide-eyed at the thought of her, ancient, travelling alone.

L'ancienne, she recalls, a term of reverence.

The well-seasoned traveller is queen for a day, before returning to truck stops and the company of her breed, where a smile or a grimace is the currency of the road, where stamina is expected, where the origin of one's licence plate is noted and the traveller granted respect in proportion to the distance. The well-seasoned traveller fills her gas tank in French. *Plein.* And whips out her thermos while handing over the VISA.

The well-seasoned traveller stops to visit old friends, and sometimes passes them by. To move on, she concludes, one cannot perpetually revisit the past.

The well-seasoned traveller makes her own routine, early rising, familiar racetracks, a favourite author. She leaves room for spirits to visit at times, to talk to her in the night, if they are civil and add to her pleasure. She is willing to entertain them, but in return, expects their loyalty in removing boors, to chase off nightmares.

The well-seasoned traveller reserves for herself the right to stop when she's tired, to bypass cairns of historic note, to trespass into towns of little remark, and notice the names on the street signs, the prices at the grocery, the condition of the produce. She reserves the right to judge critically, soundly, evaluate the colour of the table by the offerings of the market. To understand the culture by the blessings of its food.

The well-seasoned traveller will know, with a stroll down the aisle, whether meals consist of canned rigatoni, potatoes grown in Idaho, and shrivelled imports of corn from California in the middle of winter, or if the households thrive on hearty soups and homemade breads with the occasional foray into the spectacular, red peppers on shish kebabs in December. The well-seasoned traveller does not care that her inspections are peculiar, that the local IGA may teach more than a travelling photographic display from Arizona. She does not care for Arizona.

The well-seasoned traveller listens to the news of

agricultural exhibitions, rodeos, bake sales. She notes with amusement that the voices recognized as national figures are, in their home province, the same ones who announce the date and location of the annual Hadassah bazaar. Travel, she muses, both heightens and levels the perspective.

The well-seasoned traveller stops for sandlot games on the prairies, to amuse her spirits, who niggle her queenly demeanour. She purchases hot dogs to quiet them, laden with ketchup and sauerkraut. And mayonnaise. With chips. And a fudgsicle.

She checks out the pool tables in the local beverage room, dances a polka with a chubby-faced girl-child at the local oom-pah-pah fest, and removes herself to a hot bath in her motel room when she has satisfied the cravings of her spirits, and herself.

✦

Brenda

ON THE ROAD BACK WEST from Nova Scotia, a pink-striped Bronco heading east pulls a fast U-turn and skids onto the gravel by the deserted gas station where I'm walking the dog. A woman beckons to me.

A tawny cat walks the headrest, and a hand with long red nails reaches over to roll down the window.

I recognized your dog, she says.

Hey Brenda, I say, I learned to play softball.

✦

Listening to the inside of my head

I heard that my niece Maggie was being bad at the circus. She was pouting, with her back turned on her family, refusing to watch the animals. So they let her be for awhile. When she was ready, she turned back to them. Sorry, mum, she said. I was listening to the inside of my head.

I am back home in B.C. working on another election. Lightning splits the sky and knocks me off the phone. I scream at the jolt.

We re-roof the house, hanging by ropes, peeling away and resurfacing. The woman down the road fell from her roof, felt herself going, protected her head, broke her leg.

In the lightning strike, another neighbour is knocked off the phone, unconscious, shards of light bulbs filtering down over him, the lens from his eyeglasses found the next day under the washing machine one room away.

The lightning explodes wood piles and blows up the waterline at another neighbour's house. We follow the lightning ruin in the dark, by flashlight, like detectives. Charred phone line, broken windows, the long clean tear in the tree from the top to the bottom.

The next day, the sting of a yellow jacket ends my morning, high in the mountains, when the chainsaw's working and the wood is good. When I walk in my front door, I am blasted by the smell of logs, trees instead of long grass and sky outside my windows.

I hear your laughter from the other end of the country.

Last night in the dream, the phone rang early, from Ottawa the woman said she was, in that disorienting way of dreams. I don't know anyone in Ottawa.

I'm calling from T.I., she said. I have $10,000 for you.

Excuse me, I said, this line is very crackly, it's dark, I'm afraid I can't hear you well, and two skunks have got in my house. They keep rubbing against me and I cannot concentrate. Can you wait while I go to the other phone?

I'm sorry, I said upstairs, this is difficult. Two bears have come through the walls, and I don't know who you are. T.I., you said? And you want to give me $10,000? For the hospital auxiliary? For the community hall? For writing? Do you have a wrong number? Excuse me, the rain is pouring through the roof and I can barely hear you. What is T.I.?

The furry bodies wave beneath my hands, not threatening yet, but then, I have not tried to stop them. A bear passes me on the staircase, beavers push through the insulation. They don't mind me as long as I stand aside, but the house is becoming crowded, and the holes in the gyproc walls where the animals push through, grow grotesque, as pink insulation and plastic part for their entrance.

There is a lesson here, I am certain. But I don't have the sky to help me find out what it means. I don't have the ocean or the songs yet. I have a small image, of Maggie, turning her back on the circus, listening to the inside of her head.

✦

Fish story

I COULD NO MORE LIVE without writing than you could without fishing.

There is the same ebb and flow, the same flush days, the same traps to repair.

The days up at dark, when the words, or the fish, are already running; if they are not caught before dawn, they will disappear, no depth sounder, no Loran, can find them again.

There are the moments of the pure ride, sailing, bucking, the long view, and the times to dig in, eviscerate, and the days when there is simply nothing there, the waters have been plundered.

Days you are alone in the boat, cleaning the bunks, scrubbing the stove, putting the tools in order. Days you are alone with ropes to measure, bait bags and traps to mend.

There are days I am alone, months even. Years. When my cells are receptive, when even my hair senses pain, like a bad case of flu, when understanding can only be done alone, when dreams are not held off by an embracing arm, when I am restless, touchy, the days when my brain is burning. Or like you when the weather holds you back, if the work is not coming, I am nasty, hurling words.

But then when the words start moving, like Parker's quilt of fish, the solid work makes me happy. Then when it's all in place, like when the tides are full, the moon is ripe, when I have peace of mind and energy to make sense of the onslaught, then I am generous, can laugh, and write, and cook, and like the teller of a fish story, stand back, transcend, and amplify truth into myth.

✦

Dear Edwina

CAROLINE GOT MY FRIENDS TOGETHER to give me a belated 40th birthday present. It's a woodcut print of two chickens, amidst corn stalks in the sunrise, scratching the dirt. It's called "Crowing Away The Dark."

It makes me think of the day we stuffed bait bags, and talked about chickens and kids and fish and bears.

In its honour, we held a Feast of the Fowl. Caroline came with Seamus, and all my friends were there.

Before the supper, I heard how our friends in Freeport had lost their child, in an accident, on the foggy roads. And here at my home in B.C., I looked at Seamus, across the big table filled with all our best offerings, and thought of the days he comes to visit me. To talk in the sunshine, to bring me bulbs to plant, or the fresh ginger root he has pulled from the forest, still pungent and dirty from the ground, and he talks and talks using his newly found words and I don't have to say anything, he says it all for me.

He smiles at me over the long distance of the table, and I think of you there and my friends here. I think how like the woodprint you all are — you keep crowing away the dark.

✦

Heroes

IN GRAND PRÉ, we look up in a churchyard at the statue of Evangeline, to this woman who stands for the journeys of the Acadians driven from their lands.

In Preston, at the Black Cultural Centre, the map of the world traces slavery, expulsions, loyalties and settlements, the journeys a cat's cradle of lines triangulating the Atlantic.

In Plymouth, we stand before the black marble of the memorial for the men of Westray, stop breathing awhile, stand there in silence as we did during the days of waiting. Their monument is 26 rays from a miner's lamp, above the deeps where they died. Their memorial the cheques, for ten dollars or five hundred, that arrive in hand-addressed envelopes, saying to the families, you are heroes, with your strength and your anger and love for each other.

In our towns across the country each year, we light candles to the heroes we need, to the women who died in Montreal; in making them heroes, we will draw strength.

In Manitoba, on a blustery September day with blizzards coming on, I visit the Stone Angel I didn't know was real and, closer to the river, the stone for

Margaret Wemyss, Margaret Laurence, near her mother. I learn from neighbours there that Margaret Laurence was not a ready-made hero, will become a greater hero the longer she is dead, as the edges wear down.

In Alberta, I stand before the bones of dead buffalo, look out over the coulees, the short cliffs they bounded over, hear their deadness telling stories of power so unleashed it shook the earth.

Can you imagine the power to shake the earth, to take direction so firm, even while uncertain or stumbling, that you will be remembered. To take courage, not in planning or safety, but simply because that is your path?

What is this need for heroes, whose edges have been smoothed into courage, bad debts forgotten, small cruelties forgiven. Is it because their song was stronger, purer to our ears than the missed notes, the days they lay down and wept?

And I begin to understand about heroes in my life. How to transfer to the living the grace we bestow upon the dead. To hear their music purer, to accept from them their strength, and to say, in return, you will have mine.

◆